PRAISE FOR *RETURN TO YOU*

"This is a book to pick you up when you feel down and renew your hope when the world seems hopeless. Shannon Kaiser's cheerful optimism is a breath of fresh air in a time clouded by fear and uncertainty."

MARTHA BECK
New York Times bestselling author of *The Way of Integrity* and
life coach and columnist for *O, The Oprah Magazine*

"Kaiser's words encourage a deep introspection to honor our true selves and spirits."

SPIRITUALITY & HEALTH

"Shannon is so wise. She breaks feeling good down into easy steps."

JENNY MCCARTHY
actress, model, television host

"Shannon Kaiser inspires people to ditch what doesn't serve them and follow their paths to true joy and satisfaction."

MINDBODYGREEN

"Now get ready to have your life changed, and you can thank me later."

COSMOPOLITAN

"Kaiser's unique tips instantly turn stress into bliss!"

WOMAN'S WORLD

"Shannon Kaiser is an incredible woman on a mission to help people find peace, happiness, and fulfillment in their lives. Her desire to serve others shines through all of her work."

GABRIELLE BERNSTEIN
#1 *New York Times* bestselling author of *The Universe Has Your Back*

"One of the freshest voices in mental health and wellness, Shannon is on a mission to empower others to be true to themselves and live their full potential."

MARCI SHIMOFF
New York Times bestselling author of *Happy for No Reason* and *Chicken Soup for the Woman's Soul*

"Shannon transports the reader into a fascinating inner and outer journey, an unforgettable adventure of self-discovery, wonder, and awe."

REBECCA CAMPBELL
bestselling author of *Light Is the New Black* and *Rise Sister Rise*

"Now more than ever, we as women need to rise up and empower ourselves and each other. Shannon's book is like the necessary guidebook we need to get ourselves there. Self-love and inner peace can seem elusive, but Shannon has broken it down into easy-to-digest lessons."

ANDREA OWEN
bestselling author of *How to Stop Feeling Like Sh*t*

"Shannon is an expert in all things happiness, and this guidebook shows us what's possible when we remove fear and choose love."

EMMA LOEWE
editor at mindbodygreen and coauthor of *The Spirit Almanac: A Modern Guide to Ancient Self-Care*

"Shannon gives really valuable and practical information. I love it."

LEE CARROLL
channeller and author of the Kryon series

"Shannon offers easy-to-absorb advice to help you become your happiest, most loved, highest potential self. And best of all she makes it a fun process—my kind of gal."

KAREN SALMANSOHN
bestselling author of *How to Be Happy, Dammit*

"In a culture of burnout and distraction, Shannon takes you into a world of wonder where you'll transcend the trappings of a fearful mind to access your truest self. If you've been searching for your authentic path, consider this your guide."

AMBER RAE
bestselling author of *Choose Wonder Over Worry*

"There is no greater gift than allowing yourself to lean into and bathe in joy. This book gives you permission to seek and be the love that you are. I highly recommend it for those ready to dance with life."

CHRISTINE GUTIERREZ
author of *I Am Diosa*

RETURN
TO
YOU

Also by Shannon Kaiser

BOOKS:

*Joy Seeker: Let Go of What's Holding You Back So
You Can Live the Life You Were Made For*

*The Self-Love Experiment: Fifteen Principles for Becoming
More Kind, Compassionate, and Accepting of Yourself*

*Adventures for Your Soul: 21 Ways to Transform
Your Habits and Reach Your Full Potential*

*Find Your Happy Daily Mantras: 365 Days of Motivation
for a Happy, Peaceful, and Fulfilling Life*

CARD DECKS:

*Unshakable Inner Peace Oracle Cards: A 44-Card Deck and
Guidebook to Awaken & Align with Your True Power*

Find Your Happy Daily Mantra Deck

11 SPIRITUAL LESSONS FOR
UNSHAKABLE INNER PEACE

RETURN
TO
YOU

SHANNON KAISER

sounds true
BOULDER, COLORADO

Sounds True
Boulder, CO 80306

Published 2022

Book design by Linsey Dodaro

The wood used to produce this book is from
Forest Stewardship Council (FSC) certified forests,
recycled materials, or controlled wood.

Printed in Canada

BK06352

Library of Congress Cataloging-in-Publication Data

Names: Kaiser, Shannon, author.
Title: Return to you : 11 spiritual lessons for unshakable inner peace /
    Shannon Kaiser.
Description: Boulder, CO : Sounds True, 2022.
Identifiers: LCCN 2021032282 (print) | LCCN 2021032283 (ebook) | ISBN
9781683648789 (hardcover) | ISBN 9781683648796 (ebook)
Subjects: LCSH: Spiritual life. | Peace–Religious aspects.
Classification: LCC BL624 .K284 2022 (print) | LCC BL624
(ebook) | DDC 204/.32–dc23
LC record available at https://lccn.loc.gov/2021032282
LC ebook record available at https://lccn.loc.gov/2021032283

10 9 8 7 6 5 4 3 2 1

To all my teachers, mentors, and guides.

Known and unknown, seen and unseen,
past, present, and future.

Thank you.

A NOTE ABOUT RESOURCES

R*eturn to You* is a powerful process to help you connect back to your true nature. It is inspired by my own personal path to finding an unshakable inner peace even in the most turbulent times. In addition to the eleven spiritual lessons for unshakable inner peace, there are many tools to use in tandem, which I list out here.

Free "Feeling Inner Peace" Audio Meditation
I created a powerful audio meditation that you can download for FREE to help you align with peace daily. Visit: playwiththeworld.com /feelinginnerpeacemeditation/.

Discover Your Intuition Style Quiz
We all have different ways our inner guidance system talks to us, which is why I created a quiz to help you learn yours (shared on page 32). You can also access this quiz online and get an email report sent right to your inbox.
    Visit: playwiththeworld.com/discover-your-unique-intuition-style-quiz/

Questions to Ask (Journal Prompts)
Journaling is a powerful way to support self-reflection and inner growth. At the end of each lesson, I list out key questions to ask. Taking time to reflect on them will help you connect to your true nature with more peace and ease. All journal questions are listed in the Resources section starting on page 193.

Mantras
Mantras (or affirmations) are a powerful way to retrain the brain to focus on feeling good. There are key mantras shared throughout this process and book. All the mantras I mention are gathered for your use on page 198.

Life Truths

Throughout the book you will see key phrases presented as Life Truths. These are important takeaways and reflections for you to focus on through this process. You can snap a pic of them, save them on your phone for daily guidance, post them to social media, send them to your friends, or simply put them on your own vision board. The goal is to use them as tools for alignment.

Unshakable Inner Peace Oracle Cards

Using tools such as cards from an oracle deck allows you to reveal and illuminate details about your path and align to your highest good. I created an entire oracle card deck (with Sounds True) sharing principles from this core teaching and process, which is a great additional daily resource for practicing the messages from this book.

The deck includes an in-depth 144-page guidebook with clear calls to action ("Divine Assignments") and journal prompts (questions to ask, great for daily practices). Visit: unshakableinnerpeaceoraclecards.com.

Prayers

I've shared some key prayers throughout this book, and you can find a list of every prayer I've included on page 199.

Meditations

Throughout the book you will also see guided meditations to support the lessons and take the teachings deeper. You can find a list of every guided meditation shared in the book starting on page 201.

CONTENTS

Our level of love or our level of fear
determines the state of our reality.

STEPHEN RICHARDS

INTRODUCTION

can't believe this is happening again," I screamed to myself. "How did I get here?" It was the fall of 2019, and I was on a national book tour for my latest book, *Joy Seeker*. I was vibing high and really feeling the message; I was pretty much drinking my own Kool-Aid. But one night, after speaking to a group about seeking authentic joy, I was back in my hotel room and it happened—I was suddenly overtaken with panic and fear. I felt short of breath, my vision went blurry, and there were deep, gnawing pains in my stomach. I started to tear up and knew right away that this was a full-on anxiety attack. My thoughts ran rapidly in my mind; they were like an avalanche, destroying everything in their path. I couldn't stop them. I kept worrying to myself, "What if all this goes away—my dream of writing, traveling, speaking, and being of service with my teaching? This is what I live for, and what if, for some reason, it all goes away?" My ego was screaming, "Who do you think you are to live in joy when there is so much pain in the world?"

It wasn't until later that I understood that this crazy panic attack was a result of my mind's insecurities projecting my hidden fears. Luckily, I was able to calm myself down, but over the next few weeks, the anxiety attacks became my constant—interrupting my daily routine, ruining my workouts, and forcing their way into my conversations with others. Anxiety became my new normal.

One night, after yet another outburst of tears and anxious emotions, things got so bad that my entire body felt paralyzed. I knew I should go see a doctor; these panic attacks were debilitating and severely impacting my life. I screamed out in frustration, "I am desperate, I need help!" But just as I was picking up the phone to set an appointment with my doctor, it was as if an invisible force field prevented me from dialing. I heard my inner voice saying, *You can't fix an "internal" (spiritual) situation with an "outside" (physical) solution.*

And that's when I realized that my particular path was taking me deeper than I had ever gone before . . . and no amount of numbing, eating, shopping, exercising, crying, texting my ex, pill popping, doctor's visits, or panicking would save me. There had been times in my life when those things did help me—in fact even saved me, and I still believe, at times, they can be beneficial on our journey—but for me in that moment, I needed to break free from outer distractions and go on an inner journey. I couldn't hide from myself anymore.

When I started to practice the spiritual lessons that I lay out in this book, I discovered that my anxiety attacks were a manifestation of the unhealed and unbalanced aspects of me—the parts of me that were out of alignment with my true nature. Despite everything I'd learned thus far, I still had old wounds, insecurities, and hidden traumas that masked my deeper, innate wisdom. It suddenly seemed so obvious—I couldn't keep moving forward with fragments of me left behind. And so, it began: my road to recovery became a process of piecing myself back together, one spiritual lesson at a time, to reclaim my true power.

As someone who had spent the past decade teaching others how to find their happy, reach self-love, and become joy seekers (after having found these things for myself), I struggled with two questions: Why anxiety, and why now? I discovered that what was happening in my life was a personal growth battle: the outside world versus my inner world, my old self versus the emerging me, my mind versus my heart. It was time to transmute my own stuckness into wholeness, my panic into peace, and the chaos that lived within me daily into calm.

I came to see that I needed to learn what faith meant to me, and if I could truly be peaceful in the midst of the unknown and chaos of the world. I also needed to find out, Who was God to me? As you read more, you'll see that I use the words "God," "Divine Love," "Universe," "Source Energy," "Infinite Creator," and "Divine Source" interchangeably. This is my way of pointing toward the magnificent, benevolent force behind all creation. There are many names for this Divine energy, so feel free to insert whatever you most relate to. And if these words specifically don't resonate with you, by all means just feel into what is best for you. (The concepts in this book will still apply no matter what your belief system is.)

As I started to implement the spiritual lessons I share in this book, they became my guiding light and daily focus, and soon enough, things started to shift. It was the difference between being out of alignment with my true self and being in alignment. When we are out of alignment, we are often frantic, worried, consumed with fear, trying to control outcomes, and obsessing about situations. In contrast, when we are in alignment with our true self (or what I refer to as "innate wisdom" or "your true nature"), we are at ease, calm, relaxed, and in the moment. When we are in tune with the loving energy of the Universe and aligned with our highest potential self, we are at peace, no matter what is happening outside of us. Focusing on being in alignment was my new main priority, and it really worked.

LIFE TRUTH: WHEN WE COMMIT TO FEELING BETTER, THE UNIVERSE SUPPORTS US IN OUR ACTIONS.

Flash forward six months to the winter/spring of 2020, when the world was hit with a new strain of the coronavirus. Fear set in on a collective, global level, and I witnessed intense anxiety and panic every day in my neighbors, strangers, clients, and friends. I had been scheduled to go on a yearlong speaking tour, leading retreats and giving keynote speeches on stages across the globe, but within days, every single event for the indefinite future was canceled. My first thought was "*This* is what I feared six months ago! All of it *is* going away!" But I rapidly caught myself and was able to turn my thoughts around because of everything I had been practicing. I made the choice to trust in the innate wisdom of the Universe and to remain focused on my radical alignment. I did this by trusting my intuition, which helped me navigate the ever-changing new world that was emerging through all the chaos and fear.

This dynamic was interesting because we quickly stepped into one of the most turbulent times in all of human history: the entire world seemed to shut down, we encountered the most divided political landscape we've ever seen, and climate change disasters were spanning the globe. Fear was at an all-time high—the planet we inhabit was in crisis, and so was humanity. Yet amidst all this chaos, I experienced a consistent calm; so calm, even, that I felt zen, like the Buddha. My peace was my constant. As I watched other people running about in panic, extreme anxiety, fear, and worry, I realized I had learned how to embody my truest, most Divine Nature by implementing all of the practices I lay out in this book. This gave me the confidence to know that all is always in right order, always—even when it might not seem like it.

Throughout these pages, you'll see the exact steps that I took to arrive at an unshakable inner peace. Within each lesson, you will find certain key phrases that I've labeled as Life Truths—these are universal laws or pieces of spiritual wisdom that you can repeat as mantras or simply use as reinforcement for the lesson's core teaching. I also share the same tools I used to realign with my true nature, including journal prompts, mantras, meditations, and prayers. These are also gathered in the back of the book for your personal use, or to use in book clubs or group studies. All is presented with the goal of realigning you with you.

This is not a specific faith-based or religious book, but rather a process to help you connect with love in all forms, to align with what is real and true. When you have a connection to your true self and the Divine, you will be in harmony with the world. No matter what is going on outside of you, you will be able to access real inner peace.

LIFE TRUTH: WHEN YOU ARE CONNECTED TO YOUR TRUE NATURE, YOU ARE FREE FROM FEAR, AND PEACE IS YOUR POWER.

By using the eleven spiritual lessons I lay out in this book, I was able to maintain a deep calm and inner peace throughout one of the most disruptive times humanity has ever endured. I say this to inspire you, because you too have the power within you to hold the light and be the peace. No matter what you are going through, peace can be your primary state. It is my greatest wish that you become free of worry, fear, and anxiety, and step into your true path and activate your own power—the light and love within. Whether you are longing for a more fulfilling career, stronger relationships, a healthier body, or more abundance, it is all possible and much easier to attain when you are connected to intuition and love, versus fear and frustration. And when you understand the spiritual lessons available to you, you shift your energy and find yourself in a natural flow.

Chances are you've come to books, courses, classes, and coaches before, and you've tried to make things work. Maybe they worked a little, but not a lot. You've tried to apply the tools to your life, but you still feel anxious, worried, uncertain, or even just plain off. I know the feeling. I lived in this emotional state for over three decades. I tried to make things work by addressing them on the outside of me—a new diet, a new relationship, or a new creative project—all in the hopes that the successful outcome would give me what I felt I was missing. But it never did—it was always fleeting. This is why I sat down to write this book. Looking back, I realized my journey had led me through a kind of life course, because it felt as if I was taking myself through the Divine lessons to graduate into a state of wholeness. Once I discovered it was no longer okay for me to wait on feeling better, I no longer wanted to outsource my own peace and power.

The lessons in this book are a way of life. They are a philosophy to help us enjoy a deeper, more rewarding connection to our true selves and the world. Many of us struggle to see real positive change or results because we remain stuck in our past. If you have come to this process feeling hopeless, you are not alone. I, too, felt helpless and hopeless, which is why I needed a safe place to put myself back together again. This journey you are about to embark on is a safe place to help you regain trust and faith in yourself and the Universe. It will bring you back into alignment with who you really are, and from this place of wholeness, everything that does not serve you anymore—whether it is added body weight, self-sabotaging patterns or addictions, low bank accounts, toxic relationships with yourself and others, drama-filled days, or anxious tendencies—will naturally fall away and be replaced with peace and love.

What you hold in your hands are *spiritual lessons* in the form of Life Truths. This is an inspirational life guide based on spiritual, natural, and universal laws that govern all of creation. These are not only the guiding principles I use in my own life, but the principles that hundreds of coaching clients and workshop participants have applied in their lives and have seen the power of firsthand. In learning, understanding, and applying them, I've turned my life into my message. I am present, peaceful, and in love with myself and all of life. My anxiety, worry, and depression are long gone. I've lost over forty pounds (and counting) without much focus or effort. I've become completely debt free and feel calmer and more connected to myself and others. Life is much easier, less dramatic, and definitely more fun. Of course, I still have off moments and days when I feel down, but I return to the lessons in this book and bounce quickly back into alignment. These lessons can guide you forward and serve as gentle reminders that all is in right order when you activate the love inside of you, rather than leaning into fear that is outside in the world. In any given moment, we have only two choices: we can be inspired and influenced by our innate wisdom and true nature or by fear and worry. I choose truth and wisdom. Join me.

Another reason this book is so important to write and release at this time is because we are collectively shifting into a higher vibration of consciousness as we move into the new age of intuition, or in astrology often called the Age of Aquarius. As the vibration of this planet continues to accelerate, we are being called to awaken our intuitive nature. To function optimally, we need new tools. Gracefully navigating transitions, staying calm amid chaos, and turning fear into faith are not skill sets we have been taught. There is no modern road map to navigate this shift, which is why I wrote this guide—to help us all understand and accelerate into the next phase of our lives and to help bring more peace to the planet. By applying the lessons in this book to your own life, you will tap into an unshakable inner peace, which is your truest nature. I share effective strategies to help you master your own self-transformation by awakening to your inner wisdom (trusting intuition) and stepping into your authentic true power (the innate wisdom of the Universe).

Imagine having an inner faith and trust so magnificent that you are always 100 percent aligned with your true self and confident with your choices. No more worry, self-doubt, judgment, fear, or insecurities. No more shame, jealousy, or guilt. Wow, what kind of life would you live if you were operating from a place of love, kindness, and compassion for all? That is the life I wish for us all, and I know it is possible. It is why you are here; you were born with access to a steadfast inner peace, and it all starts with the return to you—your true essence and awareness of your Divine Self.

This is more than a book—it is a rallying cry, a manifesto, a call for you to tap into your inner awesome so you can shine your bright light. It's time to come together with our light, with our love, grounded in our humanity.

Over the past decade, I've studied and learned from spiritual masters all over the world. My work and perspective in life are inspired and influenced by my own teachers and guides, including Abraham and Esther Hicks; Kryon and Lee Carroll; Dr. Peebles and Summer Bacon; Sanaya Roman and Duane Packer, who work with Orin and DaBen; Paul Selig and the Guides; Taoism; Buddhism; spirituality; and lessons from *A Course in Miracles* and *The Ra Material: The Law of One*. This book in your hands is a combination of their collective wisdom guiding us to a more loving world. So many of us are seeking enlightenment or spiritual mastery from the human perspective, but once we realize our true power is our own spirit—and we shift, align, and center ourselves to that realization—our lives become softer and easier.

The foundation of the work we will do together aligns with these core ideas.

1. We are not human beings having a spiritual experience. We are spiritual beings having a human experience.[1]

---

1 Wayne W. Dyer, *You'll See It When You Believe It* (New York: HarperCollins, 2001).

2. You create your own reality through your thoughts, perceptions, choices, and awareness.[2]

3. Everything is made up of Source Energy. All energy vibrates at a different frequency. And like vibration attracts like.[3]

4. Your life is an unfolding creative adventure.[4]

When we understand and implement these core ideas, life becomes a dance, and we literally start to play with the world as we feel more peace than we ever knew possible. You are here to enjoy your life, not worry yourself through it. As you dive deeper into your own journey, trust the process and relax into each experience. Soon, without much effort, you will be living in synchronicity and ultimate flow. It all starts with you. By picking up this book, you've declared, "I want peace. I am ready to return to me."

2   Summer Bacon, *This School Called Planet Earth* (Flagstaff, AZ: Light Technology Publishing, 2005).

3   Esther and Jerry Hicks, *Ask and It Is Given: Learning to Manifest Your Desires* (Carlsbad, CA: Hay House, 2004).

4   Dr. James Martin Peebles, "The Three Principles," accessed September 8, 2020, summerbacon.com /the-three-principles.html.

LESSON 1

YOU ARE IN A SCHOOL CALLED PLANET EARTH

A childhood friend reached out to me the other day, someone I hadn't heard from in over twenty-eight years. He mentioned he was going through old boxes and had found a letter and poem that I'd written for him when I was thirteen. He sent a photo of the handwritten poem and letter, along with the message "You always know how to make people feel special." Little did he know how special it was to me that he'd sent me that note.

When I read the letter, I flashed back in time to thirteen-year-old me, the one who loved writing and expressing herself through words. I didn't know it when I was little, but I was an extremely sensitive and empathic child, so I felt into other people's energy. I always wanted to make people feel better; this was my superpower, my natural-born gift. I wanted so much to take away others' pain, and writing became the avenue through which I could do that best.

I believe we all have natural gifts that stem from what I call our true nature, that unique aspect of us that brings us immense joy and peace. For me, it has always been writing and helping people feel better. Thank goodness this is now what I do for a career as an author and empowerment coach, but it was a long, winding road to return to me.

My thirteen-year-old self didn't know this was my true essence, and fitting in and being liked became a bigger priority than liking myself or doing what I enjoyed. When I was younger, I had a learning disability that made it difficult for me to learn how to read, spell, and write efficiently, and because of this, I was almost held back a grade in elementary school. I had to take summer classes and work with yearlong grammar and spelling tutors to stay afloat. Other kids made fun of me for this. The bullying continued each year, so in order to feel safe from the ridicule, I gave up my natural expressions of self and quit writing and being there for people. By age fourteen, I had fallen away from me. It's no coincidence that my eating disorders started then, as well as my negative self-talk and self-hate.

This story isn't just my story. We all seem to have a pivotal moment, or multiple moments, throughout our younger years that shapes our adult patterns. In these moments, there are aspects of ourselves that we shy away from, hiding who we are in order to fit into the world. We fall away from our true nature.

It is no secret that we live in a world that invites us to abandon our true selves in the pursuit of fitting in. We want so desperately to be liked that we sacrifice our real self, never asking, Who am I really? For over three decades, my need to be liked and to fit in, along with my concern about what others thought about me, overshadowed my ability to be my true self. This is called the *split*: it's the moment our soul falls away from its whole self in an effort to maintain safety and the status quo.

It works for a while; we feel safe as we morph ourselves to fit the standards set by the outside world. Until it doesn't work anymore. For me, it turned into eating disorders, drug addiction, toxic relationships, self-hate, corporate burnout, clinical depression, anxiety attacks, and multiple rock bottoms. Not until I looked at this tendency to try to fit in did I see what was really happening—the quiet death of my soul and spirit.

I knew I needed to find a way back to me, but I couldn't ignore all of the experiences I had suffered through. I wanted to know why I went through what I did, and in studying Eastern philosophy and Buddhist traditions, it became clear that life is a classroom and everything is our teacher.

LIFE TRUTH: EVERYTHING IS YOUR TEACHER.

The outside world will do everything it can to keep us hooked into the "you're not good enough" narrative. For as long as we are focusing outside of ourselves on what others will think about us, or what is wrong and needs to be changed or fixed, we don't give ourselves a chance to go within and honor our true self.

I remember one day I was trapped in an intense worry spiral. I had just spent hours scrolling through social media and had caught some headlines from news channels. I normally don't watch the news, as most of it seems to be fear-based and dramatized, but on this particular day, I found myself clicking the headlines and diving deep into the dark, obsessive news rabbit hole of trauma and drama. My social media feed had been full of negativity and blame, and the news stations were spreading more doom and gloom. As I logged off, my energy plummeted. I felt helpless, but in that moment, my inner voice said, *Go to your bookshelf,* and the most interesting thing happened. I went directly to my big blue book, *A Course in Miracles.* This metaphysical text had been on my bookshelf for the past nine years, and it was collecting dust. It was nice to have it in my inspirational collection, but I would mostly pass it by and only skim the pages, never really letting the content sink in. But this day was different. My inner voice said, *Open the book!* And to my surprise, the page I opened up to was Lesson 31: "I am not the victim of the world I see." In that instant, I felt a huge wave of relief wash over me, as a calm, loving presence took over. I realized I had been giving my power away by feeling like a victim of the world, and fear had been running the show. I was focusing on the things I could not control in the outside world, and as long as I stayed stuck in that cycle, I would feel angst. It became clear to me that we don't have control over what happens on the outside of us, but we have 100 percent control of what happens on the inside of us.

As I was reading through *A Course in Miracles,* I saw how life is a course in itself. I believe our souls come to Earth to learn lessons and to grow. We can see this concept shared in Lesson 193 of *A Course in Miracles*: "All things are lessons God would have me learn."

LIFE TRUTH: WE LIVE ON THE MASTER SCHOOL OF SPIRITUAL EVOLUTION.

Sometimes the experiences we go through feel challenging because they are directing us to a new path—one that is more aligned with our highest good. It is no mistake that what you are going through is happening; you could consider it as designed for you specifically. What if your higher self and the Universe have assigned lessons for you to experience so you can learn and grow? We all have lessons and spiritual assignments in part because we are here on planet Earth, and Earth itself is like a huge classroom. From a spiritual perspective, planet Earth is one of the most difficult schools, if not the most difficult school, in the Universe, as the main lessons we receive are learned through contrast, through ups and downs. As Dr. Peebles and Summer Bacon say, we are all students of the Divine. Each experience you go through helps you learn more about yourself and those around you.

LIFE TRUTH: EVERYTHING YOU EXPERIENCE IS A LESSON, SOMETHING YOUR SOUL HAS SIGNED UP FOR SO YOU CAN LEARN AND GROW INTO GREATER LOVE.

You can discover what you are here to learn by observing the main patterns that present themselves in your life. For example, for months before writing this book, I struggled with anxiety and I was completely fear ridden. Then it occurred to me that perhaps I had "signed up" for this, in effect, in order for me to understand and grow into peace. Yep, I signed up, just like we enroll in courses at a school. Our souls enjoy learning and growing. There are endless lessons and courses we can take in planet Earth's school. My soul had signed up to learn more about anxiety, so I could then understand true inner peace. I thought to myself, *What if I choose to learn through the contrast?* By being in situations that cause angst, I could learn the power of choice, aligning with Divine Love over fear.

By realizing we are in a giant classroom and always in a learning state, I was able to quickly take my power back and understand that we are never the victims to the pains of our life, but are actually creators of the world we choose to see. It became very clear to me in that moment that not only do I have universal Source Energy around me guiding me at all times (because it led me to *A Course in Miracles* and the lesson I needed most to help shift me out of fear), but that profound teaching was available to me in that book. I knew I needed to become a student of the Course, which ultimately means being a student of life.

Over the next several months, I became a devoted student of *A Course in Miracles*. The Course's underlying premise is that the greatest miracle is the act of simply gaining a full "awareness of love's presence" in our own life. This means we can awaken to our truth, the love and power within, and ultimately return to our true self. Living a more aligned and connected life is not about roses and butterflies all the time, nor is it an airy-fairy, love-and-light process. It is a journey of deep connection to your soul, activating your Divine Purpose in each and every moment of your life. It is about accessing and aligning with Divine Love's presence so you can allow it to be a guiding force.

As you can imagine, making choices and leading from this place of wholeness feels so much better than from a place of fear. I truly believe I was able to heal myself from depression and anxiety in part by understanding the Life Truth that we are in a giant classroom and planet Earth is a school for our soul's growth. It is about the split and the shift—catching ourselves when we have split away from our self and shifting back to our true nature, the peace and love within. As we navigate our lessons in the Earth school, we begin to see that this is the journey our soul has elected to take part in, to discover and dissolve all illusions separating us from the Divine Source Energy. And like all educational experiences, this Earth school gives us plenty of opportunities to fall out of alignment so we can practice and master the return to self.

The Earth school is a school of contrast, which means we are here to experience all parts of the spectrum. We learn through the contrast; it provides clarity and power of choice. If you are familiar with the Twelve Universal Laws (not to be mistaken for the eleven spiritual lessons in this book), you may know about the Law of Polarity. This law says that everything in life has an opposite: good and evil, love and fear, pain and peace. The truth lies in understanding that these are all two sides of the same coin. If there's an up, there's a down. If there's light, there's dark. One cannot exist without the other. Experiencing these polarities is part of our human experience, and it can help us learn more about what matters most to us by enabling us to identify what we *don't* want so we can get clearer on what we *do* want.

In the book *Peace, Love, and Healing*, Mikaelah Cordeo shares this concept in more depth: "Earth's mission, if you will, is to host individuals at the maximum level of diversity of levels of consciousness . . . Each 'person or soul' is to learn to move beyond the physical, emotional, mental, and spiritual differences and to know love and honor essential Oneness . . . to lead us . . . into new levels of growth, health, and creativity."[5] Essentially, we are in a living laboratory, and our purpose is to explore contrasts through a powerful lens of perspective to lead us back to love.

I often tell my life-coaching clients to work with this law through the mantra "All contrast brings more clarity." If you're facing a difficult situation such as a breakup or a health challenge, for example, tune in to what the opposite looks like, which can reveal a new perspective. When I was hit with crippling anxiety, it became obvious to me that I couldn't truly know inner peace without experiencing such contrast. By life's design, my anxiety generated a deeper awareness and appreciation for what I was truly seeking: to feel better and more comfortable and safe in a world that often feels threatening. If we can stop looking at contrast as a bad thing and start to see it as a powerful calibration tool to help us realign with our own truth, then we can balance ourselves and expand in the beautiful opportunities and move past all stress and struggle.

---

5   Mikaelah Cordeo, *Peace, Love, and Healing: New Teaching from Lord Jesus the Christ* (Mount Shasta, CA: Golden Rose Publishing, 2015), 80.

LIFE TRUTH: IF WE REALLY WANT TO UNDERSTAND AND KNOW SOMETHING, WE MUST KNOW THE OPPOSITE.

The ancient Chinese philosophy of Taoism focuses on the principles of yin and yang, signifying the balance of life. The contrast is rooted in understanding peace.

Verse 22 of the Tao Te Ching shares:

> *If you want to become whole, let yourself be partial.*
> *If you want to become straight, let yourself be crooked.*
> *If you want to become full, let yourself be empty.*
> *If you want to be reborn, let yourself die.*
> *If you want to be given everything, give up everything.*

The idea is that we must be willing to explore all aspects of life in order to truly know ourselves and grow. This new perspective can shift us into a place of self-compassion and more love.

We are here to discover more about ourselves through the experiences we have. You may be thinking, "Wait! I didn't choose this troubling situation!" but from a spiritual perspective, it's possible your soul did. Mikaelah Cordeo dives deeper: "We choose pain and suffering so that we might be inspired to make better, healthier choices, and sometimes, so that we might more deeply understand the underlying reasons that caused others to choose in these ways."[6]

These experiences are all lessons. We learn lessons in fear, grief, depression, powerlessness, insecurity, unworthiness, jealousy, anger, blame, worry, frustration, greed, power, anxiety, hopefulness, acceptance, surrender, compassion, happiness, purpose, joy, passion, appreciation, freedom, unity, and so much more. When we understand we are in a big classroom and everything on planet Earth is an opportunity for us to learn, we can relax more and trust the journey.

---

6   Cordeo, *Peace, Love, and Healing*, 83.

As students, it then becomes a question of, What "class" do I want to take?

Take for example my friend and coaching client, Maz. She was born in Manila, the capital of the Philippines, into a poor community comprised of tin sheds and houses patched with magazines and newspapers. Throughout her life, she struggled with financial security and was even homeless for a while. But she learned how to transform her life through accepting contrast and understanding that she advances in life when she learns the lessons presented to her. By committing to not remaining a product of her past, she became a fitness model, landing a two-page spread in *Oxygen* magazine, then tapped deeper into her spirituality. Today she is a Law of Attraction teacher and speaker. She even wrote a book that became a bestseller in Australia. Through embracing the contrast and being willing to learn the life lessons available to her, she learned firsthand how to go from zero to becoming her own hero. We hear stories like this all the time about people born into extreme conditions of abuse, poverty, or famine, who turn it around by understanding their soul's personal lessons and freeing themselves from their circumstances. It is empowering to know that we have more power over our experiences than we've often believed.

In knowing that everything on planet Earth is an opportunity for us to learn, we no longer need to take things personally or feel like the Universe is attacking us. Once we understand this, we discover it's all an experience we can elect to participate in. We can release the burdens of feeling off track or behind. And most importantly, we can realize we are not being punished. Living with this awareness can help us surrender more in the present moment of life and embrace each situation as it comes. We soon see that everything is part of the balance of existence.

William S. Burroughs is credited with saying, "When you stop growing you start dying." New lessons and new opportunities for growth are always available to us. The best thing we can do is let go of the idea that there is a *there* to get to and focus on the here and now. You can do this by identifying what lesson you're currently learning. What class have you enrolled in? And are you learning through the lens of lack or love, fear or faith? One thing that has helped me on my journey is to constantly seek out where I have fallen away from my true nature, and I do this through the lens of honesty and being willing to learn the truth.

The lessons we learn are all opportunities to come closer to the truth. In Ram Dass's book *Polishing the Mirror*, he says, "It is important to honor your own truth even though to other people it may appear inconsistent."[7] I am constantly asking myself, "What is true for me? What am I learning? What is the lesson here?" And with this commitment and dedicated focus, I continue to grow and align back to my true self. Here is a mantra you can say to help support you through each life lesson: "I am committed to discovering my truth, and I trust the process. I welcome life lessons because they represent growth."

As we advance through each class on our Earth school, we can recognize that each one of us has our own soul work to do and no two lessons are the same. We all come here to learn through our experiences, but based on our own soul's journey, we will each need different lessons and will live through different experiences. This is why you may have an entirely different memory of your childhood than your siblings or friends; we each experience life through our own lens and our own thoughts, which is why others may see the world differently and have a different perspective on their past. If another person has a totally different approach to life than yours, it could simply mean that they are here for different lessons, but together, you can help support each other's growth.

Since everyone and everything can be your teacher, having different soul lessons from those around you doesn't have to be a source of conflict. When we lead with compassion and respect, we can support one another on our personal growth journeys. The easiest way to do this is to make choices from your heart. When you filter life's lessons and all experiences through your heart, you are honoring your whole self: your heart, mind, body, soul, and spirit. As Ram Dass shares, "What is most important is where you are doing it from—that is, your point of view.

---

7   Ram Dass with Rameshwar Das, *Polishing the Mirror: How to Live from Your Spiritual Heart* (Boulder, CO: Sounds True, 2013), 47–48.

Are you doing it from your ego, your role, your personality? Or from a place in you that doesn't change—your spiritual heart, your soul?"[8]

Imagine that you have a magic wand and are granted one wish! Your higher self, or maybe a hot genie, pops out of a bottle and says, "Hiya, Gorgeous! Your wish is my command." What if, instead of wishing for that one thing to make your life better, you wished to learn all your life assignments through joy, peace, and love? Because let's get honest. You've been wishing for that *same* one thing for decades. I know I did— the ideal number on the scale, the soulmate relationship, financial freedom. What if you wished to remain connected to your true self and to Source Energy forever more? If you truly hold these intentions, all of those other things you want will naturally fall into place.

The goal, then, while living your life with more grace and ease, is to accept all your assignments with open arms and an open heart. When you do, you see your life has so much purpose and you are here for a reason (and a season, as you will learn in the next lesson). Let this reason drive you forward. What kind of life do you really want to live? What life lessons would you like to enroll in on this big, beautiful school called planet Earth?

As we close out each lesson in the book, I will present clear action steps that you can take to put each lesson into practice in your own life.

Let's put this lesson into practice:

The following steps can help you apply what you've learned so far and dive deeper into this grand, glorious school called planet Earth. To activate this lesson, You Are in a School Called Planet Earth, try these steps.

Step 1: Detach from drama.
The more you can disengage from the drama happening outside of you in the world, the easier it is to go inward and focus on your own healing. So often the world tries to pull us in different directions. Daily demands and to-dos can keep you from being fully present on

---

8 Dass and Das, *Polishing the Mirror*, 47–48.

your journey. Instead of giving your attention away to these outside forces, declare, "Peace is my priority and I detach from drama." Begin by paying attention to what you are consuming—what you watch on TV, what you read on social media, who you listen to for advice. What you consume will ultimately consume you, because we always get more of what we focus on. Be aware of your thoughts and intentions. Stop focusing on what is going on out in the world, and instead focus on your inner world and actively choose peaceful thoughts. Cultivate kind thoughts and see fear for what it is: a distraction and an illusion that tries to manipulate our reality.

Step 2: Go on an inner awareness adventure.

We frequently get overwhelmed by frustration over what is or isn't happening in our lives. You may feel like you aren't where you are supposed to be, or that things aren't going the way you want, but recognize that there is a universal plan always at play. The lessons you are learning as you go through each experience are powerful moments of inner growth; but as long as you keep focusing your attention on the outside world, you will stay stuck. The only way to truly heal and bring more peace to your life and the world is to invite more love—and that love lives inside of you. If you feel overwhelmed by the world and what is happening in it, focus for a moment on your inner world. The Law of Consciousness states that our outer world is a reflection of our inner world. So if we see chaos, fear, and uneasiness out in the world, we have an opportunity to look within and recognize the uneasiness within ourselves. When you focus on what you can control—your inner world—you will have more moments of peace. And with each moment you can focus on being in gratitude for what is going well, you will soon see how nothing outside of you can hurt you, especially when you are aligned with love.

Step 3: Seek your truth.

The next step is to be discerning with all things and seek the truth. When you are aligned in integrity with your intuition, you will see things clearly. You may break free from things that used to pull at your attention or try to manipulate you. Begin to question things you used to accept as normal, such as your routines, habits, limiting thoughts—even your job, relationships, or cultural conditioning. Observe all situations that no longer feel good. Practice using more discernment as you look at the world around you—you might get a sense that things are not what they seem. This is part of your own life advancement as you observe and study the lessons available on Earth.

LIFE TRUTH: INNER GROWTH CHANGES YOUR REALITY.

As you ascend to a higher vibration and the next phase of your life, all things that are not aligned or in integrity will fall away. The more you learn about yourself and the world, the more you start to trust yourself, and with this comes a driving need to seek out realness and authenticity. You will demand it from yourself and others, and you will start to see that fear is an illusion that manipulates your reality—and you will no longer want to engage in it.

Step 4: Commit to being a student of life.
It's extremely helpful to release the need to get to a destination and instead see your life as an ever-unfolding adventure where your choices are part of the reward. Each choice you make leads you in a new direction, one you can embrace with love and joy. By committing to a life of learning, you allow your soul to grow, and you proudly show up for all the life assignments you encounter. It is no longer about the goal or achievement but about living, exploring, allowing, and experiencing. By going into all situations and asking, "What is the lesson available to me?" you learn and grow with more grace and ease. Instead of trying to get to a destination and bypass all of the learning, you relax more into the journey. By committing to be a student of life, you embrace each experience as it is, and you begin to see how profound your life can be.

Questions to ask:

1. What is the lesson and course I am currently in?

2. How can I participate more fully in my own growth and inner expansion?

3. How have I learned through the contrast, and what is true for me?

As you complete the lessons your soul needs to learn, you will grow into what I call the next-level you. Every next level of your life will demand a refreshed version of you, and the next lesson will guide you through the process to align with this optimal aspect of yourself. This next lesson will help you amplify this energy and step into your true nature, the internal peace within.

LESSON 2

IF YOU DON'T GO WITHIN, YOU GO WITHOUT

In September 2020, Oregon (the state I live in) was hit with devasting wildfires, which spanned over 900,000 acres and displaced over half a million people, who were forced to evacuate their homes. At least five full towns were completely destroyed. The Pacific Northwest is usually a wet climate, so Oregon had never experienced anything like it. Countless people, including some family friends, lost their homes. With so much devastation and chaos, it was hard to stay grounded and connected to peace. Everywhere we looked, it was catastrophic. I felt like we were in an apocalypse movie; the sky was tinged blood orange and filled with thick smoke, people wore hazard protection masks, and sirens blared all around the cities. For several days, we had the worst air quality on the entire planet. We literally couldn't breathe! The smoke began to take a toll on my health. I had chronic headaches, my nose and throat were scratchy, and I experienced disjointed thoughts and brain fog. For a few days, I even felt a heavy pressure in my lungs. I wanted to drive to cleaner air or book a flight to escape the horrendous conditions, but I'd have been driving for days, and all flights had been suspended due to the hazardous conditions.

We were stuck in the chaos. The world around me was in complete disruption—but as I came to see, that didn't mean my inner world had to be. Still, my first gut instinct was to panic. My anxiety raced back in as I thought about worst-case scenarios: losing my home to the fire—or worse, losing family members—or having permanent lung damage. As I frantically paced the house preparing to pack up items in case I had to evacuate, it occurred to me that I had a choice. In each moment of panic, I could pause, and in that power of pause, I could always seek to align with peace. With nowhere to go outside, I had no other choice but to go inward.

I knew this was an opportunity to go on an inner journey into my heart. I was put on notice; my inner world needed tending, too. This is commonly referred to in spiritual circles as "the work"—the deep spiritual journey that all of us are destined to experience. When we commit to a life of personal growth, we will always be presented with more opportunities to do our inner work. But rest assured, you will always be rewarded for this deep healing. On the other side of the work is pure self-compassion, joy, love, forgiveness, and ultimate inner peace.

Although inner work is often one of the most challenging things we experience, it reaps tremendous rewards. So many of us are terrified of doing our inner work because we aren't sure what we will find. Hidden fears, old patterns, and beliefs that are sabotaging us lurk in the inner realms of the subconscious. In the decade I've been coaching and leading workshops, I find that people tend to fall in one of two categories: those who think their problems will be solved by looking outside of themselves, and those who are willing to look inward for solutions. The latter group often has tried looking outside of self for years and has realized it doesn't work. The outside world can't give you the solution to what is going on within.

LIFE TRUTH: WE CAN'T SOLVE OUR PROBLEMS WITH OUTSIDE SOLUTIONS; LASTING RESOLUTIONS ARE ALWAYS SOLVED BY THE WISDOM WITHIN.

One of our fundamental needs as human beings is to be deeply heard, acknowledged, and understood. But so many of us look outside of ourselves to fulfill this need. We chase and climb until we realize that no amount of outside quick fixes can heal what must be nurtured on the inside. Once we understand this, wanting to know more about ourselves and our inner world is what paves the way for the inner work to happen. As Kryon says in many of his messages, "Truth reveals itself when you give the intent to know more."

When the fires in Oregon, on top of statewide lockdowns for COVID-19, forced many of us to stay indoors, I used that time to go on an inner journey and discover more of my deeper reasons for being. One thing I noticed was that my emotions were like a tsunami—waves of sadness followed by relief, worry, and frustration. I allowed myself to feel them in each moment, which was new for me. I used to do everything but feel my feelings. I would hide them, push them away, and deny their value. I did this by overeating, overworking, overspending, overexercising, isolating, using drugs, trying to maintain control through my eating disorders, and escaping in any and all ways possible. My feelings were frightening. But in this new reality, my feelings became my friends. Jess King, a self-love advocate and Peloton fitness instructor, says emotions only last five to six minutes max. If you can hold on and then ride it like a wave, you can always move through it. And sure enough, this was my experience, too.

One night I felt really balanced. I had just finished a great workout and I was cooking a healthy meal. I went to put on music while I cooked, and within seconds of the first song that played, I felt an overwhelming force of sadness rush over me. It hit like a tidal wave of grief, and I could do nothing more but fall to my knees and weep. I cried heavy tears of sadness for the state of the world, the families who had lost their homes, and the helplessness I felt—all of it pouring through me, releasing in the warm, wet tears. I sat with it and allowed it all. I didn't judge my tears but invited them. These feelings were important to feel. Instead of trying to work or distract myself from them, I embraced them. Sure enough, within a few minutes, the tears dried up, and I felt a sense of relief wash over me. A healing presence set in, and I knew I had transmuted my sadness into love. Then my inner voice said, *There is more you can do. You are not helpless.*

After I felt my emotion of sadness, I could move gracefully back into my true nature—one of love and peace—which gave me insight to be of service and help in more ways. I felt inspired to help those who had been directly impacted by the wildfire. I went around my house and gathered food items and new and lightly used clothes to donate. I went to the store and bought care packages of toiletries and socks for families in need. I donated all proceeds that month from my meditation albums to nonprofits collecting for the victims of the wildfires. I woke up each morning with the desire to help and be of service, and all of this happened because I felt my feelings. If I hadn't allowed myself to express the sensations, I would have still been stuck in overwhelm and sadness. My brain and heart would have never arrived at a place of support, solution, and action. But feeling my feelings was the key to coming back into balance.

Sure, we may have periods of our life that feel dark and depressing, but within those periods can be moments of hope, happiness, and release. Similarly, if we feel good and are riding high on the joy bubble of life, unexpected anxiety, fear, and frustration can often creep in—and this isn't a bad thing. It is the whole spectrum of emotions that makes our life rich and rewarding. Judging or denying our emotions only keeps us from fulfillment. If we refrain from judging the feelings and allow them to be as they are, we can move through them and transform them. This is where our true power lies: in our inner world. In understanding your feelings and letting them guide you, you can transform your entire experience.

LIFE TRUTH: OUR EMOTIONS ARE GIFTS; WHEN WE ACCEPT THEM TO BE OUR GUIDING LIGHT, THEY LEAD US TO OUR TRUTH.

In Sherianna Boyle's book *Emotional Detox: 7 Steps to Release Toxicity and Energize Joy*, she states that feeling our emotions is key to help flush out negativity and clear a path for new positive habits. She says, "There is only one emotion, love. Everything else is a reaction."[9] The emotions we feel are reactions to situations we experience. My sadness was a reaction to the wildfires and worldwide catastrophe and health crisis. The only real, pure state is one of love. So when I felt the feelings and allowed them to move through me, heal, and be released, I could then return to my state of wholeness.

We aren't taught how to express ourselves through emotions, but this is built into our DNA and human function. In fact, society will often tell you to hide your feelings, using statements such as "Suck it up," "Big girls don't cry!" "Be a man, don't show emotion!" or "Don't be such a baby." This common vernacular gets drilled into us at a young age and disconnects us from experiencing the real, raw human experience. But we have it backward.

LIFE TRUTH: OUR EMOTIONS ARE GATEWAYS TO OUR HIGHER SELF AND A DIVINE CONNECTION TO SOURCE ENERGY.

When you allow yourself to feel, you open up your energy field to access the Divine Wisdom available to us all. In the teaching of Taoism, the heart is your message center. We can connect to love through our heart. It is not the everyday human ego (stuck in the head) self, but a deeper self—your true self, the innate wisdom within. True self *is* a state of peace, while the ego self is easily agitated and disturbed by life. The true self *is* love, while the ego self feels a lack of love, which is why it is constantly seeking love and acceptance from outside sources and attachments. When we go within our heart, we can allow the true self to be our full self.

Choosing your true self is choosing alignment with the Creator. At any moment of any day, you have a choice to align with your true nature or not. When you choose this path, you activate your heart center,

---

9   Sherianna Boyle, *Emotional Detox: 7 Steps to Release Toxicity and Energize Joy* (Avon, MA: Adams Media, 2018).

and the connection to wisdom and intuition is ignited. When acting from fear or unprocessed emotions, we feel frantic and panicked, but by aligning with our true selves, we can make choices from love, which is calm, connected, and more spacious. Always ask, "Will this bring me peace or take away my peace?" and make choices from the place that helps you feel most whole. And if you don't know which choice is best, you can always say this prayer:

A Prayer for Discernment

Dear Source,

Please guide me to the path of least resistance and optimal alignment.

Please help me see the truth and connect to the outcome that is for the highest good of all involved.

When we move from fear back into peace, we are essentially moving from mindlessness to mindfulness. I recognized this lesson firsthand during the wildfires. I had no control over the world outside of me, but I could control my inner world. I invited a presence greater than my own to fill my heart, and I realized that we are always right where we are supposed to be, and God will put us where we need to be. When we realize this, there is no real need to worry because worrying only projects our minds into the unknowable future and distracts us from possibilities; but in the present, we can find peace. And in the moments our ego tries to convince us otherwise, we can remind ourselves that right now we are safe. And in each moment, we can feel and express love.

The ego analyzes; the Holy Spirit accepts.

A COURSE IN MIRACLES

By returning to my true nature, the unshakable inner peace within, I could connect to Divine Love in each moment. We each have this inner power to connect to the truth: love is our protector, and no matter how much chaos is happening out in the world, it is within your inner world that you can take refuge or inspire action. I accepted what was happening in the world instead of trying to judge, resist, analyze, fix, or control it. I relinquished control and accepted this as an aspect of life. I started to repeat a message in my mind inspired by the teaching of *A Course in Miracles*: "If this be of God, there is nothing you can do to stop it, and if it is not of God, it will come to naught." This passage helped me slip into a deeper surrender. If all that was happening was the will of the Creator, I had no choice but to allow and invite in the experience more fully. I could stop trying to play God by letting my ego attempt to control my circumstances and instead just be at peace with God, which meant being at peace with all that is.

> Peace is the result of retraining your mind to process
> life as it is, rather than as you think it should be.
>
> WAYNE DYER

The late spiritual teacher Wayne Dyer wrote extensively on this topic in his book *There's a Spiritual Solution to Every Problem*. He shares, "When we are connected to God, we have no problems . . . What we need is a change in thinking to realize that a connection to the divine good, or Spirit, or God, is what heals or eradicates our problems."[10]

As we recognize that all of life's problems are pathways to greater understanding and that they invite us closer to Source Energy, we can begin to release any long-held shame and guilt. After we give ourselves permission to feel our feelings, it's much easier to release judgment, shame, and blame. I let go of my judgment and worry about the world and accepted the turbulent situations for what they were. Can you look at the world without adding anything to it—just

---

10   Wayne W. Dyer, *There's a Spiritual Solution to Every Problem* (New York: HarperCollins, 2001), 16.

see it for what it is? Can you let the world be the world instead of trying to change it or fix it? When we resist or try to change what is happening, that is when the stress takes hold. Instead, I allowed. And in full acceptance, peace became my regular state.

No matter what you are going through right now, you can detach from drama by returning to the present moment and centering yourself. Lesson 190 in *A Course in Miracles* says, "I choose the joy of God instead of pain." This became my mantra through the devastating months of the wildfires and the pandemic. Any time fear, frustration, or overwhelm set in, I turned my attention to love. I trusted that there was a loving, benevolent force greater than any temporary experience occurring on Earth, and with this force for good surrounding me, I would make it through.

By making it a habit to go inward and listen to my heart, I also had a chance to hear my intuition more clearly. We each have a guidance system so incredibly powerful and strong that it can lead us through any and all situations. It is not outside of us but within—our intuition. It is that "gut feeling," the inner knowing that we all have but so often ignore. This is what I call innate wisdom and refer to often throughout each lesson.

When was the last time you found yourself in a situation that didn't turn out the way you hoped, only to have that inner nagging voice say, "I told you so"? We tend to ignore the red flags and warning signs in the beginnings of situations. Whether it's a job you know you don't really want or a relationship that seems too good to be true, we tend to override our intuition with analytical thinking, but this is a trick of the ego and mind. Your analytical mind wants nothing more than to keep you safe, and it attempts to do that by overstepping its domain. The intuition is the voice of truth and reason, and although your ego believes *it* is truth, the only real truth is derived from your heart. Only when you start to access the Divine Wisdom of your heart, which is your intuition, will you see how manipulative the ego has been. The ego's illusion is shattered when we listen to and trust our heart.

LIFE TRUTH: THE MORE YOU TRUST AND BELIEVE IN YOURSELF, THE FASTER THE EGO SUBSIDES.

I used to rely only on outside information and advice. If I had a dilemma, I would ask everyone I knew what they would do in that situation. I would often listen to all the advice, but with so many different opinions, they often drowned out my own. I was always confused and frustrated. I would take others' advice because I didn't trust or believe in myself. The truth was, when I listened to others, my choices felt forced, and it watered down my experiences.

On the flip side, one of my close friends, Veronica, used to always ask me for advice and never take it. Several years ago, I remember getting mad at her one day because she started asking for more advice on a situation, and I burst out, "You didn't listen to me last time, so I don't know why you ask for advice then don't take it." But I see now how wonderful it was that she didn't take my advice, because no one knows what is best for you more than you. She ultimately would trust herself and listen to her intuition.

Sometimes we ask others for their opinions, but it doesn't mean we have to do exactly as they recommend, because their advice is meant to serve as a compass to steer us back to our true north. It's totally normal to connect with others and ask for their opinions, but your inner knowing is the best compass for you. Today I don't really ask for advice from others, for I know I am my own best guide, and that my connection to Source Energy and my intuition are the strongest tools I have for navigating life.

Learning the language of our heart, our intuition, is one of the best practices for accessing daily peace. One of the questions I get asked often in workshops and coaching programs is "How do you get in touch with your inner guide and trust it?" I always say, "Get to know your unique intuition style." We all have different ways our inner guidance system talks to us. In my retreats, I share a process I created to help us understand the language of our inner guide. You can take this fun quiz to learn yours. Or take it online here: playwiththeworld.com /discover-your-unique-intuition-style-quiz/.

HOW TO DISCOVER YOUR INTUITION STYLE

1. **How do you learn best?**
   a. When the info is written or sketched out and you can see it
   b. When it is spoken/listened to/via audio and you can hear it
   c. Through personal experience—your feelings
   d. When you research, learn facts, and dive deeper into your own knowing

2. **How do you make decisions?**
   a. Visualizing the outcome/making vision boards
   b. Talking about it/listening to others' advice and guidance
   c. Gut feeling, inner knowing
   d. Based on past experience

3. **When you watch a great movie, what do you remember most?**
   a. The scenery/cinematography, visual effects, costumes, etc.; how it looks
   b. The soundtrack (your digital music library is full of soundtracks)
   c. How it made you feel
   d. The storyline, the characters, and the acting

4. **What do others/friends say about you?**
   a. You help them see things in a unique, new way
   b. You're a great listener and always there for them
   c. You give excellent advice
   d. You are loyal and trustworthy

5. **When you communicate with others, how do you respond to let them know you understand?**
   a. I see what you mean
   b. I hear you
   c. I feel you
   d. I know what you mean

Now add up your answers to reveal your intuition style.

Mostly A's

You Are Clairvoyant—Clear Seeing/Inner Seeing
Your intuition speaks directly to you in the form of sight. It is your dominant sense, and you may see images in your mind or interpret information through pictures. You have the ability to see events from the past, present, and future in your mind. When people speak to you, you may see images to interpret what they say, and you learn best by seeing and experiencing. Your life is like watching a little movie inside your head. You see things unfold, and each image guides you on the right path.

Signs You're Clairvoyant:
- You daydream often.
- You see clearly how things fit together.
- You have a deep connection to beautiful things.
- You have a vivid imagination.
- You envision plans in your head.
- Your sense of direction is on point.
- You have vivid and intense dreams/daydreams.
- You're a creative person.

Exercises to Improve Your Clairvoyance Skills:
- Sit quietly with your eyes open. Breathe in and out steadily.
- Focus on an object in front of you, such as a plant, crystal, book, coffee cup, etc. Make sure it is a still object and won't move.
- Continue to focus your attention on the object but start to increase awareness of your peripheral vision.
- In your mind, take note of the objects and furniture around you.
- If you see shadows, sparks, or movement, keep focused on the item in front of you.
- Sit for as long as you feel comfortable (usually 3–5 minutes).
- Make notes/journal on what you saw and felt.

- To increase your clear seeing ability, do this exercise often. Pay attention to any internal vision that took place and changes in your awareness.

Mostly B's

You Are Clairaudient—Clear Hearing
Clairaudience is a way of receiving intuitive messages without using your physical ears but rather hearing messages within your mind. Your higher self, Spirit, the Universe, talks to you through your ears. When clairaudient abilities are beginning to open up, you may notice ringing in your ears, changes of pressure in your ears (such as popping or buzzing noises), or you may start to hear voices. Don't worry, you are not going crazy but rather opening up to your intuitive channel. Think of clairaudience as an inner hearing. For example, you may suddenly hear that little voice inside you say, "Go right!" or "Stop!" Trust it; this is your intuition guiding you.

Signs You're Clairaudient:
- You talk to yourself often.
- Sudden inspiration or ideas just come to you.
- Growing up, your best friends were imaginary.
- Music makes you feel connected to your soul.
- People come to you for advice and support.
- You hear ringing or high-pitched noises in your ears.
- You learn through the auditory channel.
- You can "hear" animals.
- You hear whispering, noises, talking, or radio in the distance.
- You hear messages that sound like they were delivered just for you.

Exercises to Improve Your Clairaudience Skills:
The easiest way to develop your clairaudience is to practice sensitizing your hearing.
- Go to a place where you are comfortable and at ease. I love to do this exercise in nature.

- Close your eyes and take a few deep breaths in and out.
- Set the intention that you want to improve your intuition and connection by increasing your psychic hearing.
- Relax your body and let hearing be your main focus and dominant sense.
- Gently tune in to sounds that you don't normally focus on. What can you hear? Perhaps birds chirping, squirrels running, maybe wind brushing through the trees?
- Really pay attention to the layers of sounds and feel into each new vibration.
- Document your findings in a journal or audio message you record for yourself.

Try this exercise in several locations, and journal on the experience. Stretch yourself and try your intuition style in different directions and with different focus.

Mostly C's

You Are Clairsentient—Clear Feeling
Clairsentience is the ability to receive intuitive messages via feelings, emotions, or physical sensations. Empathy (feeling the emotions of others) is also a form of clairsentience. You get all your information via feeling or sensing subtle energies around you. People who are clairsentient can sense others' emotions and easily pick up on energy.

Signs You're Clairsentient:
- You feel drained after being in a large group of people.
- You have awesome instincts about people, places, and situations.
- You sense energy in the room.
- You can immediately tell when someone is having a bad day (even when they are smiling).
- You find it difficult to watch the news.
- Emotional movies leave you in tears.

- You feel emotions (not your own) randomly and seemingly without cause.
- You are super sensitive to your environment.
- You physically feel other people's pain (physical and emotional).
- People say you're too sensitive.
- You have strong gut feelings.
- You can't shop at thrift or antique stores.

Exercise to Improve Your Clairsentience Skills:
People who are clairsentient are sensitive to changes in energy. This is one of my favorite exercises to strengthen my clairsentience. I use this five-step approach:

- **Step 1:** Ask a friend or family member to show you a picture of someone they know very well but you've never met.
- **Step 2:** Look at the picture and feel into it by observing all aspects. Try to focus on the person's eyes and try to tune in to the energy of this person. Focus your energy on how this person was feeling when the picture was taken. Was this person happy? Disenchanted? Relaxed? You may feel a burst of energy, such as stress. Note that if this is the first time you're practicing clairsentience, you may just pick up basic negative or positive vibes. But the more you do it, the easier it will be to feel into the energy.
- **Step 3:** Ask yourself what kind of person this individual is. Would you trust this person?
- **Step 4:** Share your findings with your friend.
- **Step 5:** When you're done, ask your friend for feedback. How correct were you? You can repeat this exercise as many times as you want.

Mostly D's

You Are Claircognizant—Clear Knowing
Claircognizance is the ability to just know something without logic or facts. It may help to think of it as an inner knowing. For example, if you know that you shouldn't trust your new neighbor or go down that street at night, but you don't know why, that is claircognizance. Claircognizant feelings can be very strong. They can also come in the form of intuitive thoughts that can pop into your head at random. This is often the most mistrusted or misunderstood of intuitive abilities because there is no real evidence, just an inner pull. The ego mind will try to convince you it is not true, but your heart and inner knowing has certainty; you know the truth. Always trust it.

Signs You're Claircognizant:
- You spend your time thinking a lot or writing a lot (many authors and songwriters are claircognizant).
- You have lots of sudden ideas that you can't wait to share, often keeping you up at night.
- You look at new ideas with a skeptical and analytical mindset.
- You are a creative ideas person.
- You frequently have déjà vu.
- You can always tell when someone is lying.
- You know when someone is genuine and trustworthy, often with no explanation.
- You are the answers person. People ask you to help solve something they can't solve—a personal issue, a work issue, a logistical issue—anything, really.
- You prefer learning through books or written works.
- You trust things you can't see.
- You know what the outcome of a situation will be before it happens.

Exercises to Improve Your Claircognizance Skills:
The best way to amplify your inner knowing is with automatic writing.

In the beginning of your intuition development journey, it's normal to second-guess yourself and wonder if the "gut feelings" are real. But automatic writing allows you to know for sure the messages you are receiving are trustworthy.

Here's how to do automatic writing:
- **Grab a pen and pull out your notebook.** Before you start writing, ask your higher self a question, such as
  - o   What guidance do I need today?
  - o   How can I find resolution to a problem?
  - o   How can I be of service today?
- **Then set a timer for five to twenty minutes, and write whatever comes to you.** Don't edit yourself or worry about spelling, grammar, or even legibility—just write.
- **Express yourself fully and write whatever comes to you without thinking about it.**

The more you do this exercise, the easier it will be. Trust yourself and the messages you receive. Our intuition is always working with us. It is up to us to develop a plan to increase communication. Much like exercising to improve your health, you can improve connection with your Divine Wisdom by practicing these tools daily. Our brain gives us an opinion, whereas our intuition gives us truth and knowing, which are accessed through the heart. As we start to trust our inner guide, we can see that everything is connected.

LIFE TRUTH: LIFE IS A MIRROR REFLECTING YOUR INNER WORLD.

What is happening out in the world, outside of you, is not separate from you, but is rather created, invited, and accepted by you. The world we see is a filter reflecting our innermost thoughts. It's no coincidence that everything is connected. I saw the connection when I applied this Life Truth to the destruction happening on the West Coast with the extreme forest fires. So often we think that problems are happening outside of us, but we would not be able to see or participate in the problems if they were not a reflection of something within us.

At the time of this writing, there was extreme chaos across the world, especially in the US. Whether it was mass shootings, political unrest, police brutality, race wars, protests, exposure of human slavery and suffering, major injustices, media manipulation, climate change, or domestic terrorism, it felt like we were always under attack. In the disgust and confusion following such events, we often fall more deeply into despair and fear. We feel hopeless and powerless against the negative forces in the world. But I thought to myself, *What if this is an opportunity to take more responsibility and be accountable?* These events, and in fact all terror-inducing events on planet Earth, are a manifestation of the deeper spiritual issues affecting all of us. It's an invitation to dive deeper into the underbelly of what is happening as a result of any chaos. Yes, there is pain, separation, trauma, and fear out in the world, but it couldn't exist if it weren't also present in our inner world. *A Course in Miracles* says, "Your outside world is a reflection of your internal state." In applying the lesson of this chapter—If You Don't Go Within, You Go Without—we can see that everything is connected and that we have a role to play in the world we see. In every experience, we can ask, "What is this bringing up for me?"

When I saw the chaos and pain out in the world, at first it gave me great offense. Terrorists were hurting innocent people, fires were burning people's homes, and family and friends were arguing over who was a better presidential candidate. The separation was ripping us apart. But when I held up the energetic mirror, I asked, "Where is the separation within myself? Where are the injustices within my own life? Where am I living in chaos in my own life? What flames and rage do I have within?" We don't have control over what happens out in the world, but we have full control of our inner world.

When uncomfortable and challenging events happen, it is easy to point fingers and place blame. But by pointing the finger outward, we still participate in the problem by being part of the problem. Our true self, the God-like self within, knows no separation. All of the push and pull is a desperate cry for the return to love we crave. If we take a proactive approach, we can see how we are all here together and how we are connected. With all the pain and turbulence on the planet, there is an even greater opportunity for love, both for ourselves and for one another.

LIFE TRUTH: WE MUST DO THE WORK OF OUR INNER WORLD TO HELP HEAL THE OUTER WORLD.

As Carl Jung said, "Everything that irritates us about others can lead us to an understanding of ourselves." When we look within our own hearts to see the connections in events, we start to see that we have more power than we previously realized, even in what often feel like powerless situations. Sure, we can continue to look outside of ourselves while blaming and pointing fingers at others (it's my ex's fault, my mother-in-law will never understand, my boss is the problem, that client is the issue, the president—or the ex president—is to blame, etc.), or we can focus on how the situations are not actually "separate" from us but within us.

When we push against what is and blame outside situations for how we feel on the inside, we are victimizing ourselves and removing ourselves from unity. All this does is pull us into more fear. Fear would like nothing more than for you to be separated from others, so it is easier for you to be controlled by it. If we are honest with ourselves, we can see the part of ourselves that we have split away from or denied. Most of the pain isn't from what's happening out in the world, but what is going on within ourselves: the subconscious recognition that we are acting from a place separate from our true nature, the Divine Love within. Many of us are in pain and hurting, full of inner turmoil coming from the emotional terrorists in our own minds. We may not attack others, but we condemn ourselves, and we judge ourselves and others, especially those who don't agree with us.

We walk around not feeling good enough or worthy of our own desires, or we feel more important or better than those around us. Then, when destruction or real-world threats happen, we feel even more trapped and helpless. We beat ourselves up for not being further along in our journey or not feeling better, especially when we believe that we should be feeling better—that we *should* know how to do everything after all the books we've read and the coaches, courses, and classes we've taken. By staying stuck in these frantic thoughts, we continue to push connection and love away. We separate ourselves from the flood of infinite well-being. For so many of us, our inner world is filled with hate, sadness, disrespect, and frustration, yet we continue to look out into the world and think the problem is out there. It's time we reversed this.

LIFE TRUTH: WHEN WE FOCUS ON HEALING OUR INNER ANGST, THE OUTSIDE WORLD CHANGES.

Instead of panicking, worrying, or blaming the outside world, I stabilized my inner world. Lesson 34 in *A Course in Miracles* shares, "I could see peace instead of this." I began to pull all my attention to possibilities and peace instead of destruction and harm. I looked at the imbalances within myself and committed to healing them. After making this commitment, within twenty-four hours my entire experience shifted. Not only did I wake up with a calm awareness, but the constant pit I had felt in my stomach for weeks was replaced with peace. I woke up to rain, which we desperately needed to fight the wildfires. The air quality had improved dramatically overnight. All of these felt like major miracles. Now, I am not saying my positive focus created all this, but I am saying that because I focused on positive outcomes and began to clean up the anger, hate, and shame within myself, the world outside of me began to reflect back a more loving, hopeful experience—one of balance, harmony, and peace.

When you change the way you look at things,
the things you look at change.

WAYNE DYER

We can choose peace, but it must start on the inside. You can access freedom from fear right here and now. No matter what is happening outside of you in the world, your inner world is the only world you truly have control over. It is your everything.

Let's put this lesson into practice:

These steps will help you implement the lesson If You Don't Go Within, You Go Without.

Step 1: Judge nothing that occurs.
Deepak Chopra said, "If you and I are having a single thought of violence or hatred against anyone in the world at this moment, we are contributing to the wounding of the world." When the world seems to be turned upside down and nothing makes sense, it can be so easy to fall into judgment and blame. With so much angst, there can be a lot of separation. Adopt a mentality of compassion and kindness by practicing nonjudgment and compassion for all. Today, practice nonjudgment with everything you see. As you live in a more neutral state, watch how aspects of yourself and your life start to feel better.

Step 2: Drop from your head into your heart.
Our thoughts are powerful directives. They will either help us or hurt us, depending on where we give our attention. The mind will analyze, judge, blame, and try to make sense of the world, but your heart trusts, allows, and loves. There is no point in trying to change the world, but there is a point in changing your thoughts about the world, and this happens when you drop from your head into your heart.

It's often been said that our thoughts create our outcome, so if this is the case, we must ask ourselves what we are thinking and projecting about the current situation. If something is causing you dis-ease, go inward to your heart and see what your thoughts are about that situation. Feel your feelings and recognize where you've been trapped in fear or blame. We can escape our pain by giving up all thoughts that are derived from attack, blame, or shame. We are never trapped in the world we live in, because as soon as we shift our thoughts, we can change our experience.

Step 3: Hold up the energetic mirror.

Look at what is triggering you and causing you distress. Hold up the energetic mirror and ask yourself, "How is this showing me what I need to heal within myself?" Your external world is a reflection of your internal state, mirroring the deepest truths of your soul. Use this time to recognize all areas and relationships and situations that feel strained. Heal your past by connecting to it in the present. You have a Divine Assignment to not take things personally. Look at who and what is triggering you and what it is bringing up for you. When you feel your feelings, you release them, and as you do, you connect to the deeper message they can bring. Using the energetic mirror will help you reconnect with your true self, the pure light and love within.

Step 4: Build your intuition.

You have an inner superpower that will guide you to safety, freedom, and the path that is always for your highest good—your intuition. Learning how to trust your inner voice instead of listening to the conflicting and fear-based voices of the outside world will help you feel peace faster. Think of your inner voice as the voice of truth and reason. It is a direct channel to your higher self and higher power. Its loving guidance will always support you. Develop a plan to increase communication with that part of yourself. As you start to trust your inner guide, you can see that everything is connected.

Step 5: Turn your resistance into assistance.

Instead of resisting things in your life you don't like, channel all the energy into assisting. Where can you help others and turn your pain into purpose? Go inward and ask yourself, "What is coming up for me?" When we first help ourselves, we have the capacity to then help others more fully. You can stabilize your focus by assisting others after you yourself are tended to. Sometimes we don't have control of what is happening, but we can help those in need. Being of service is the highest form of happiness and will help you stay focused on the big picture—that we are all in this together and need each other.

Questions to ask:

1. What is my intuition style, and how will I grow my connection to it?

2. How's the outside world mirroring my inner world?

3. Where do I feel called to help and be of service to others?

Once we have learned the power of our emotions and connecting to our heart, we start to feel more peace and purpose. And by learning how to trust your intuition, you will see that you are always safe and protected when you align with love. Soon you will start to witness more beliefs and perspectives that have been limiting you, and it will be time to move past them. In the next lesson, you will learn how to transform your experience of life by shifting your focus so you can align with your true power, Divine Love.

LESSON 3

FAITH IS FREEDOM FROM FEAR

I used to suffer from chronic overthinking. I took life pretty seriously, and although I've always been a glass-half-full kind of gal, after the West Coast wildfires, I went through a mini phase of extreme paranoia. In the weeks following the event, I found myself rabbit-holing down a deep, dark path of doomsday predictions. Everything from potential volcano eruptions or major 9.0 earthquakes that were long overdue on the West Coast (the geologist lectures on YouTube said so, so it has to be true), tsunamis, meteor strikes, killer bugs, more pandemics, nefarious leaders with dark agendas, robot takeovers—every day was filled with "What is going to rear its ugly head today and try to harm us?" When the alien invasion started to be a very real possibility in my mind, I realized all logical reasoning had gone out the door. I was deep in it, manipulated by conniving fear, all under the guise of "I am being prepared and educating myself." I told myself I was getting ready for the next big thing that could happen, not realizing that this was full-blown fear that had manifested itself into a preparation project.

I naively thought that if I learned more about all the possibilities, then when and if something unexpected did happen, I would be set. This was a sneaky ego trick, manipulating my mind into fear under the guise of *safety*. Since I didn't have control over anything outside of me and the world seemed unpredictable and chaotic, I convinced myself that at least I would be prepared for whatever the world would throw at me. Then I could control my response in any outcome, especially if I had all the bases covered. So, when and if any of these so-called catastrophes happened, I would be ready. My ego could say, "See, I told you so. Good thing you listened to me!" And our ego loves nothing more than to be right.

But all of this frantic energy was causing enormous stress on my body and life. I gained weight, I was lethargic, the stress changed my body chemistry, my skin kept breaking out, and I had major digestive issues, not to mention a constant knot in the pit of my stomach. This was the result of chronic overthinking. Lo and behold, the anxiety found another way to creep back into my life. Each day, the more research I did, the more possible scenarios I uncovered—but the more I tried to control and learn, the more helpless and hopeless I felt. In our hopelessness, fear can fester. It wasn't until I went out to dinner with some friends that I saw how much fear had manipulated me.

As my friends and I were catching up, they asked how I was doing. And I gasped, "Over the past few weeks, I've been in a constant state of worry. I go to bed each night, and I let out a huge sigh of relief thinking how great it was to make it through another day without a catastrophe—only to wake up in the morning holding my breath and thinking to myself, 'Oh crap, is today the day the earth will implode?'" I mean, I was kind of joking, but not really. My life was consumed with doomsday predictions, and I didn't see the madness of it until that moment when I said it out loud and saw the reactions on my friends' faces—there it was, the look of my being cuckoo crazy. And that is what our fear is: ludicrous (and not the cool rapper kind). It was then I realized how much fear had taken over my life. They laughed uncomfortably, but the look in their eyes said it all; they were looking at me like I needed to check myself before I full-on wrecked myself. I felt like a caged animal at the zoo. They were on the outside looking in on me and my isolation—while they were free. Free of fear, free of worry, free of the anxiety-induced coma I had put myself in. It wasn't until I went home that night that I realized the previous few weeks of my life had been full of worry for no good reason. Fear had hijacked my life, and I needed to take it back.

This is fear's endgame: to kidnap truth and keep us in the dark, disconnected from truth and love. It doesn't matter whether we are worried about pandemics, natural disasters, our partner cheating on us, or how we will get out of debt or lose weight—all fear is manipulative and deceiving. It completely distorts our reality, making us feel like we are being protective and smart, yet completely destroying all connection to the moment and to real Divine Love.

So many of us latch on to the ego by trying to take charge of our own life in an attempt to buy ourselves safety. But the illusion of safety is a projection of our ego. It's a trap that is designed to keep us under its influence of duality as a form of separation from Divine Love. When we release our attachment to the ego, we see the true avenue to security and freedom is to surrender every area of our life to love by leaping into our faith with conviction. With this commitment comes a new reality, a way of living that is free from judgment, shame, and criticism. As we allow love to lead, it becomes the central experience of each moment, and we live with more ease, joy, and peace.

What blocks us from feeling love's presence and the safety that comes with an inner knowing that all is well are the ideas from the mind—and information in our mind can overwhelm us. We are all, to some degree, suffering from information overload. We are bombarded daily with information about the world out there, what is happening (and usually about what's going wrong). Whether it is social media, news, gossip, or conversations, we are constantly taking in new information. A lot of the information is fear-based misinformation, created to evoke responses and keep us sucked into a low-energy state so we can be controlled and manipulated. My friend Christine Arylo wrote a whole book on this topic. In her book *Overwhelmed and Over It*, she teaches that one of the root causes of feeling overwhelmed and off balance is the system we live in: "Your internal system has not been conditioned to handle the amount of information coming at you, nor the accelerated pace and intensity of today's world, so you keep short-circuiting"[11]—aka burning out and resorting to overwhelm and fear.

---

11 Christine Arylo, *Overwhelmed and Over It: Embrace Your Power to Stay Centered and Sustained in a Chaotic World* (Novato, CA: New World Library, 2020).

But if we want to align with our true nature and awaken to our true power, we must detach from this fear-based, information-overloaded world and step into serenity—and we do this by aligning with faith, which gives us freedom from fear. When I say faith, I am not pointing to a specific religion or doctrine; in this lesson and throughout the book, I point to faith as a commitment to love.

When I was stuck in my doomsday delusions, I reached out to my dear friend and mentor Summer Bacon, who works with Dr. Peebles. I shared my concern about the current state of the world and possible situations that could unfold. Because fear was still in the driver's seat, I recognized that I had separated myself from love's calm presence, and in my frantic state, I needed a fresh perspective. They reminded me how important it is to stay connected to our true nature and make all choices from this loving place:

> *Don't take actions that would steer you towards fear. You want to stay in a place of truth and trust, for God and humanity. And trust that God will put you where you need to be at any given time, and you will know exactly what you are supposed to do at any given time—there is no need to panic and go to fear, it is unnecessary.*

It became obvious to me that it is all about intention. I can fill my day with worry and fear-based thoughts, or I could choose hope, happiness, and love; I could unplug from the "system," stop consuming so much fear-filled media, and instead drop into my heart.

The presence of fear is a sure sign that you
are trusting in your own strength.

A COURSE IN MIRACLES

It's important to think about how you feel with the information you have and activities you do. Do you feel energized and calm, or frantic and in fear after watching, listening to, and participating in them? When fear is in the driver's seat, we have yet to recognize that our mind is participating in the illusion of separation. We have forgotten the Divine Source as the true strength that will always take the place of our weaknesses. The instant you are willing to see this truth, you realize there is nothing to fear.

Paul Selig, a prolific author and speaker who channels the Guides, spoke about this important distinction in one of his Freedom from Fear workshops. He said, "You cannot be a victim and master at the same time." When we are in fear, we are victims of our life situations, but to be one with love is to be in alignment with the Creator, which shows you are the master of your own life experience. In the workshop, he teaches:

Fear breeds fear, every choice you make in fear will give you more fear. But the true self lifts what it encounters. It's a vibrational resonance—when you are being true to yourself you uplift those around you. The only true problem of humanity is the denial of the divine. Understand that the divine is the only truth. What you put in darkness calls you to that vibration. So how do we not get pulled down and stuck by the shadows? It's very simple: know who you are (remember the God light within). Understanding source is present in all things and moves you into action. Everything must be re-known that of Source.[12]

The realization of the divine in all things isn't something you make so but something you align to.

PAUL SELIG, THE GUIDES

---

12   Paul Selig and the Guides, "Freedom from Fear" workshop, Berkeley, CA, April 7, 2018.

To understand fear's role in your life, think about how often you feel helpless versus empowered. Helplessness and hopelessness are side effects of being in the victim role. The writer Azrya Cohen Bequer breaks down the distinction in an easy way:

Victim Consciousness says,

> *"I have no or very little personal power. I am at the whim of my external reality, and things are happening to me beyond my control. My fear-based Ego must cling to any semblance of control it can find in order to ensure its survival, and fight for that control at all costs. I project blame externally, refusing to take responsibility for my reality."*

Creator Consciousness says,

> *"I am infinitely powerful, precisely because I am ready to relinquish my false sense of control and trust in the greater intelligence of life (and death) itself. Everything I experience— pleasant or not—is a result of some form of conscious or subconscious co-creation. It is through taking full responsibility for my experience that I liberate myself from victimhood."* [13]

The truth is we are the manifestations of our own life experience. Are you living from victim or creator awareness? We always have a choice. Do I succumb to the current operating system of "victim consciousness"? Or do I claim my "creator consciousness"? Truly, each moment, each one of us is being confronted with the decision of which operating system to run. When you align with your faith, you are free from fear.

Love is the great protector.

RA, THE RA MATERIAL: THE LAW OF ONE

---

13   Azrya Cohen Bequer, "What Psychedelics Told Me about the Coronavirus," Medium.com, March 23, 2020, azrya.medium.com/what-psychedelics-told-me-about-the-coronavirus-730a4a6b9714.

We can access this benevolent power by being more of our true self. Our true self is one of love and light, and we activate this loving energy when we stay centered in our alignment with Source. Start by first detaching from your fear-based thoughts. Fear blocks us from seeing the truth, and most of our fears are not based on reality but on projections in the mind. Therefore, our thoughts are often the barriers blocking us from feeling more grounded and at peace.

When I was trapped in my frantic fear phase, my ego was trying to play God. I was striving to control the outcome by predicting what "would or could" happen, striving desperately to prepare for all scenarios, and in doing this, my ego was loving every second because it was acting as God. The ego wants to be in power. It is its greatest wish and its ultimate endgame, as it constantly rearranges itself to fit a narrative that keeps you separate from love's embrace. The ego loves to fight against *what is* by making you feel as if you are the one in control and in charge. This is why we feel so bad when we are living from our ego. Self-doubt, judgment, and shame don't feel good, but we stay in this place because it is a false safety; we may feel secure in our insecurity, but it is an illusion. Choosing love is the way forward. Your faith is the bridge to this way of living. Essentially, all thoughts are protections or reactions. We get to choose whether they are inspired by love or fear.

When we are in fear, the real reason we are upset is because we have distanced ourselves from the truth, which is that we are one with the love of Source. Our thoughts are separate from the Divine. We can direct our thoughts into a deep abyss of self-suffering, doom, and gloom, only perpetuating the worst-case scenarios, or we can direct our thoughts back to love, unity, kindness, joy, and compassion. In each instant, we have this choice and option to reclaim our power. I started to do this by repeating, "My thoughts about my deepest fears are not my reality. They are illusions separating me from love." I repeated this often, returning to the present moment.

Fear lowers our vibration and takes us out of the here and now. How are you spending your moments? You can gauge where you are in any given moment by how things are flowing in your life. Do you feel peace, love, abundance, freedom, health, or joy? Or do you feel frustration, anger, fear, overwhelm, confusion, or franticness? There's no wrong feelings or wrong way to live your life, but I have found that choosing to rise into a higher vibrational state (one of love and joy) is far more rewarding—not to mention it takes less effort.

LIFE TRUTH: YOUR TRUE ESSENCE IS MADE FROM LOVE, WHICH IS YOUR NATURAL STATE, SO IT IS EASIER TO BE WHAT YOU ARE THAN TO RESIST IT.

We spend so much time resisting our own light because fear is what we learn. Fear is a lower vibration; it takes more energy to stay there because our true self resides in a higher-vibration resting state. This means when you are in fear, you have to work harder to stay there. This is why fear feels heavy, and when we are consumed with worry, we often feel exhausted and anxious; plus it can weaken our immune system and fog up our reality. But often, when you are in joy and happiness, you have more energy, you feel lighter, and time seems to expand.

Think about the last time you did something you absolutely loved. It felt good, and you were probably able to sustain that activity for a long while because it gave you life force and purpose. So the fix to fear is to start shifting to love by doing more of what you love. I was able to bounce out of my pathetic panic parade by doing what I love—which is writing, creating, and helping others. I channeled all my worry energy into new articles and blogs for magazines and wellness websites, and I created a new meditation album called *Fear Detox*. I created the *Unshakable Inner Peace Oracle Cards*. I stopped resisting and started to assist. I returned to my true nature and became a creator. The more I stepped into my faith with love and intention, the more I transmuted the fear.

No matter what you have been feeling, you can shift in any moment into a new, more loving vibrational state. Making this choice, one of committing to love, will demand more of you. Staying in fear is safe because it is expected and known. The collective unconscious of humankind is one of fear, so to break away requires the courage to show up for the light; but once you embrace it, ease always ensues. At first, it will ask more of you because you are breaking away from the herd mentality, but as you do, you will find freedom and a magnificent flight of the soul—for this is your true essence, and it is always worth it. It requires radical faith. Faith is believing in what you can't see but knowing it to be true.

Carl Jung, one of the founders of modern-day psychology, was interviewed for the BBC before he passed away. During the interview, he was asked whether he believed in God. Jung responded, "Believe in God! No, I know."[14] When we know, we are in full alignment with our inner light, which is connected to truth. And truth is undeniable. Faith aligns you to what is real: love. It's not about a religion or specific doctrine to follow, but as a spiritual life truth, it is about aligning with what is true.

Since we are diving deep into the aspects of fear, there are times in our lives when we feel like we really are in danger, and our worst fears can become our reality. Even in difficult times, faith will free you from fear. I have a coaching client and friend, Chanelle, who took a trip to Brazil to meet her close friend who lived there. As they were driving through the countryside to visit a nearby beach town, they came upon a large concrete block that was strategically placed on the highway. The sun had just set and because it was darker, her friend didn't notice the block until it was too late and ran over it, which damaged the car and blew out a tire. As the car rolled to a stop, two men rapidly approached their car with guns and started banging on the windows and yelling, "Get out! Get out!" The doors were locked, so one of the men used the guns to smash the windows.

Chanelle told me her story and explained how time seemed to stop, and for the first time in her life, she was fully present in the moment. Although it was a terrifying experience, she did not go into fear. Instead, she prayed with every fiber of her body, "Dear God, please guide me. Please help them have a change of heart. Please be with

---

14   John Mundy, *Living A Course in Miracles: An Essential Guide to the Classic Text*, (New York: Sterling Ethos, 2012).

us and them." As the men tried to pull her out of the car and steal their belongings, she continued to repeat this prayer; it was her solace. Her prayer gave her peace, and she remained calm. She surrendered deeply to the moment and trusted the Divine fully by diving deeper into her faith.

Chanelle felt God's presence and kept repeating her prayer, and then something miraculous happened—she saw something in the man's eyes shift. The man who had been pointing his gun at her and who had been yelling profusely in her face, so close she could feel the spit burst on her forehead, suddenly ceased his yelling. His eyes turned from cold, remote, and angry to soft and gentle, and he released his hold on her while putting his gun down. He went to his friend, then came back to her and said, "GO!" Then the two men ran off with only their material goods and left Chanelle and her friend unharmed, and they were never to be seen again by her or her friend. The two miraculously made it to safety in a car that was basically totaled. As she relived her story and shared with me, I was in shock that she had experienced such a traumatic event, yet she had remained calm and peaceful. She said, "My faith is stronger than fear. It saved me." She went on to share, "I truly believe that God has us go through difficult things as an invitation to bring us closer to love."

For so many of us, life will continue to deliver unexpected and often traumatic events. Each one of us has a different way to process such experiences, and of course I'm not discounting those raw feelings that need to be felt and expressed, as it's not always easy to get past fear. But even in the most horrific situations, we can find peace in our heart when we trust the Divine. Faith tells us that we are protected in the Universe by Divine Love, so fear cannot really exist when we are focusing on the power of alignment.

It is from your peace of mind that a peaceful
perception of the world arises.

A COURSE IN MIRACLES

We can choose peace, but it must start in our mind and heart. Our ego will try to convince us that the outside world needs to first become calmer, and only then can we find peace. But our true self, the spiritual self, knows that once we find peace, everything outside of us will be in harmony as well. One of the best ways to build up a solid foundation of being in alignment to Source is by raising our energetic frequency.

Here's my go-to list for overcoming negativity and fear by raising your vibration.

Feel Your Feelings

First recognize that feeling emotionally low is not bad. So often we feel that when we are depressed, sad, or anxious, there is something wrong with us. But this is, in fact, just part of life. The denser emotions are the energy sources that can give us clarity and help us learn more about ourselves. As I shared before, when you feel your feelings, they can transmute and heal.

Sage

You can create a sacred energetic space by setting an intention for peace and harmony and cleansing a room—or your whole house—with birch bark, sage, or essential oil spray. Rituals such as sage-burning or using incense, also known as smudging, are a powerful way to do this. Sage is derived from the Latin word *salvere*, which means "to be saved." Aside from the metaphysical uses of smudging, research has shown that sage can also be used to benefit physical, mental, and emotional well-being. Note that from a high-vibrational standpoint, you want to make sure all the ingredients you use are sourced as sustainably and respectfully as possible. The rise in popularity of smudging white sage in particular is threatening supply, so you can always consider a smudge spray or an essential oil diffuser instead, which is what I use.

Crystals

Since ancient times, crystals have been used for their powerful energetic healing properties. These rocks, gems, and stones can help heal deep-seated issues, bringing forth good health and greater happiness.

Each crystal has its own unique healing properties, and because they are from the earth, they have a profound healing energy inspired by nature. This earth energy is also grounding and can help protect against negativity.

My favorites for raising my vibration:

Black Quartz comes from the Himalayas, a spiritual sacred ground, which increases its healing powers. It will defend you from any kind of psychic attack, and it will keep you away from harm on both physical and psychic levels. The healing energies of the black quartz will cleanse and purify you, as well as the environment you are in.

Citrine is another go-to. It helps absorb negative energy while bringing positive energy into your space. It can help you develop a more positive mindset.

Rose Quartz is the queen of self-love. It can be helpful for those who suffer from depression because it is so comforting. This crystal brings in soothing and healing energy to the heart chakra and helps you be gentle to yourself and develop self-love.

A Prayer Practice

No religion required for this one, but if you are religious, this method may be your sweet spot. Spending time in "prayer" simply means connecting to a force and power greater than yourself. (This can be God, the Universe, the Divine, Allah, Elohim, Jesus, Buddha, Ganesha, Tao, Infinite Creator, Source, Higher Self, etc.) Prayer can be a powerful practice, as it helps get us out of our head and into our heart. Prayer also helps us by bringing us a sense of meaning and purpose, as it is something that connects us to hope and joy and makes us feel connected to the world around us. Don't underestimate the power of prayer. Sometimes we feel helpless and as if nothing we do will make a difference, but praying helps us connect to something much larger than ourselves. It requires radical trust because we can't really see what we are praying to; but knowing that our prayers are always answered can help us in each moment.

Hot Bath with Epsom Salt

My number one favorite self-care activity is hot Epsom salt baths. The minerals in a detox bath are believed to help remove toxins from the body to improve your health, relieve stress, and connect you back to your true self. Not only is it soothing, relaxing, and joyful, but it is a way to show yourself more love.

Essential Oils

Lemongrass, lavender, and sage oils are powerful healing oils to help calm the mind and relax the spirit. You can use a diffuser, inhale them, or apply them topically. I also put them in my bath for added relaxation and instant *ahh*.

Meditation

Meditation is just the act of being so fully present that your worries can't exist. My meditation practice looks like doing what I love. When I write, I feel calm, centered, and in the flow. Doing what you love is a powerful form of meditation because it helps you center within yourself and return to your true nature.

Listen to Your Body

Your body has innate wisdom and infinite ways to communicate with you and help you through situations. Our bodies are magnificent teachers. Start to listen to yours, including the types of food it craves and when it feels out of balance. Ingest high-vibe foods. Natural, unprocessed foods help me feel best, and when I eat organic foods and drink lots of pure water, my body thrives.

Move the Body

We often hold negative feelings in our bodies, so dancing, walking, and exercising are all great ways to release that energy. Moving your body is an important part of healing.

Feed the Body High-Vibrational Foods

What you put in your body directly impacts your vibration. Foods from the earth make us feel better. No matter what diet lifestyle you prefer, adding more high-vibration foods—foods that come from the earth and are grown with sunlight and water—will nourish your body and assist with detoxification.

Earthing

Earthing is the act of connecting with nature: walking barefoot on the ground, feeling the grass, or literally hugging a tree. One of the quickest ways to lift your mood when you're feeling low vibrational is to get outside. I know when I was depressed, some days it was hard to make it out of bed, but when I stepped outside and breathed in the fresh air, I always felt better. You can always open a window to let fresh air into your space—or better yet, physically go outside, because escaping from your current environment can calm your mind and ground you. Nature is a natural mood lifter that connects you to the peaceful vibrational consciousness of our planet.

Use Mantras and Oracle Cards

Think of mantras as if they were your psychological wellness center. They fill your mind with positive, healthy, motivating thoughts, and in turn, they flush out toxic vibrations and low-vibe negativity. Oracle cards are also a great tool to help you align with each moment. You can even check out my *Unshakable Inner Peace Oracle Cards*, which I created as a supportive tool to supplement the teachings in this book.

Explore Your Passions and Do More of What You Love

Doing what you love not only raises your own joy levels but also puts more love out into the world. You have gifts, skills, talents, and passions that are important to you. Trust them, honor them, live them.

Create

To be human is to create, but most of the time we think it needs to turn into something to be of value. But the sheer energy and exploration inherent in the act of creation itself is the true magic and joy. Creating can be writing, painting, dancing, cooking, gardening, or having a wonderful conversation with someone. Find ways to be creative with your time and energy, and start a creative project just for the fun of it.

Seek Positive and Truthful Information

In the past, when I felt blue, I went to positive websites, blogs, and YouTube channels. I sought out uplifting messages and tools to help raise my vibration. Finding a consistent source of good vibes can help you feel more balanced. Reaching for feel-good information that is grounded in truth, integrity, and education often requires that you be willing to dig deeper than the mainstream news, as much of that is drenched in fear-based lower vibrations. Align with yourself by seeking more uplifting and empowering content.

Cuddle Sessions with Furry Friends and Loved Ones

Calling a friend and reaching out for support is important, but sometimes just taking time to cuddle with your furry friend or loved one will transform any negativity and help you feel better fast.

Fear will often try to take over, but it helps to recognize that we all have bad days and that fear doesn't have to be our normal way of living. We don't need to define ourselves by a bad mood or the fear thoughts that creep in. Seek to raise your vibration and step away from fear.

This is by no means a full list of things you can do to raise your vibration, but it gives you some ideas to test out. If you are having a hard time feeling better, try any one or all of these tips to help pull you into a higher vibration. Furthermore, you can tap into inner peace by knowing that you are surrounded by Divine Love always. Love is around you always and available to help. We can remember that the Creator created us and all things, and that everything we see is part of this Source Energy. This is love in action.

Let's put this lesson into practice:

To activate this lesson, Faith Is Freedom from Fear, try these steps.

Step 1: Alchemize your fear and unprocessed anger.

Our emotions can be transmuted to a higher plane—much like the process of turning base metal into gold—to become powerful and transformative forces in your life.

Our base emotions are simply energy that has been trapped in reactive and protective defensive patterns. As a collective, fear, anger, and hatred have been programmed into our society as our reality and our go-to emotions. Whether it is fear of an invisible virus coming to attack us or hate stemming from systematic racism, we are all experiencing these base emotions, which are reactions to perceived danger, violation, or hurt. But within each emotion is a more loving, higher emotional state—a nonreactive state that can respond with appropriate love and intelligence to the various circumstances of life.

When fear is transmuted, it opens you to the quality of love. Pain transforms into lovingkindness and compassion. When we practice this alchemy, these emotions will transmute into positive power and love and ultimately lead us to true inner peace. You have a light inside of you that is magnificent and loving. It trusts life and believes in the power of possibilities. If you've been stuck in frustration or worry, chances are that fear has hijacked your consciousness. It is time to reclaim your true Divine Self. Do this by alchemizing your fear:

Guided Meditation to Alchemize Fear

1. Identify Your Fear

Start by feeling the fear and sitting with it. The things you are afraid of can be your greatest teacher. Name your fear. What is the fear at the center of your current experience? Fear of being judged, not being loved, not being accepted, dying, losing loved ones? Identify the fear and call it out specifically.

- Where does it live in your body?
- What does it feel like and look like?

Really feel into the fear and be present with how it feels. By identifying it, you no longer run from it or allow it to control your experience.

2. Step into Your Fear

Imagine this fear engulfed by a tornado of energy. The fear is now circling and rotating in a fierce motion all around you. The fear has become a tornado of energy. Step into the center of the tornado and allow this fear to override everything in its natural frantic pace around you. Do this visualization and energy work until you are at the peak of the fear. Really feel the intensity.

- What does it feel like?
- What emotions are coming up?
- What is your natural response to this experience?

Do you want to run, fight back, or hide? This is an indication of where your power, or lack of power, lives—and where you've been giving it away.

3. Understand Your Fear

The next step is to stay present, centered in the middle of the tornado of energy and frantic fear, and understand it. You do this by working with it and communicating to release its energetic hold and power over you. Stand in the tornado and really feel the movement and energy. As you do, stand firm in the center and ask these questions:

- What message do you have for me?
- What are you here to teach me?

4. Transcend Your Fear

This next step will help you embody this fear. Understand that this fear is an illusion. It is a false identity and thought form that has been given to you from outside of your true self. Take your power back by aligning with your truth. In this space, stand firm in the center of the tornado of fear and repeat three truths. In between each truth, say, "I disengage with all illusions. I am not separate from my truth. I am love."

It looks something like this (although you will create and repeat your own truths):

Truth one: "In this moment, I am safe and secure."

Mantra: "I disengage with all illusions. I am not separate from my truth. I am love."

Take a deep breath in and out.

Truth two: "I am willing to see the love available to me in this experience."

Mantra: "I disengage with all illusions. I am not separate from my truth. I am love."

Take a deep breath in and out.

Truth three: "I am a child of Source Energy, love, God, etc. My power is in my connection to the Divine."

Mantra: "I disengage with all illusions. I am not separate from my truth. I am love."

Take a deep breath in and out.

Your truth is your power. When you actively participate in disengaging with emotions that are bringing you down, you can reclaim your power and help to uplift not only yourself, but the entire world.

* This meditation is inspired by an original teaching in the book *Busting Loose from the Money Game* by Robert Scheinfeld.

Step 2: Reclaim your creator focus.
A Course in Miracles teaches that God is not the author of fear—you are. When you are in fear, you have chosen to create away from God. We can either be in victim mentality or in empowered creator consciousness. Choose to align with the Divine, and know that you are always safe with the connection to the love in your heart.

Step 3: Surrender to your faith.
Know that only peace and joy are the final outcomes for everything. A lot of the anxiety we feel is tied to not knowing what the outcome will be. Anxiety is a fear of the future, and the unknown is one of our greatest fears. But when we put our faith in God, we trust the unfolding and see that all is always well and all is in Divine Order. If you are feeling worried and unsure about the outcome, turn your fear over to the Universe, and remember that joy is your birthright and cannot be denied to you. You can be at peace, and all is well when you trust and put your faith in the hands of the Divine Creator.

Questions to ask:

1. How can I focus more on the moment and appreciate all that is going well?

2. How can I relinquish control of the situation causing me the most stress?

3. What is my fear, anxiety, worry, or discomfort trying to show me?

4. How can I reclaim my power?

5. What is my faith asking of me?

When we move from our ego mind (mindlessness) to our heart center or higher self (mindfulness), we step into a higher quality of life. We switch from ego to spirit, from fear to love, from being protective to receptive. Allow your faith to be your guide and release you from the perception of the ego mind so you can embrace true peace and freedom. However, we cannot let go of the illusion if we do not know that we are in one. That's why the next lesson is dedicated to helping you break out of the illusion and dream state caused by your limiting beliefs. We will build upon our solid foundation of faith and begin to understand where our beliefs are hindering us. In the next chapter, I will show you how you can radically change your results in life by shifting your beliefs. It's one of my favorite lessons because it shows us how to break free from all limitations. Let's dive in.

LESSON 4

YOUR BELIEFS CREATE
YOUR REALITY

After my last book, *Joy Seeker*, came out, I started sharing excerpts, quotes, and teachings from the book on my social media channels. Several months after the book's release, the world fell into a dark, traumatic, devasting time with the onset of the worldwide pandemic. There was so much heaviness, sadness, anger, and fear that joy almost seemed impossible, like it was too much to ask for. I could tell that many people believed we don't have a right to joy when there is such injustice and pain in the world. But I knew the exact opposite is true. Joy is our birthright and responsibility, which I knew firsthand because my own commitment to love and joy had helped me to feel better and stay calm through such chaos. I felt called from a soul level to be a beacon of light and to spread hope by being a positive force in the world. If I committed to joy and stayed out of fear and negative thinking, I could help to uplift others as well.

So I resolved to be intentional with every message I posted on social media, but my efforts were not always welcomed. For instance, there was one account I followed that used astrology, gematria, and translations of ancient texts to make predictions. I reached out to the page owner in a private comment thanking him for his daily posts, only to have it majorly backfire on me. The person never responded directly to me, but instead screen-grabbed my profile and posted it publicly to his page, along with a caption that was a complete lie. He said, "This account and people like @ShannonKaiserWrites [my Instagram account] may seem innocent, but don't be fooled. She is a dark witch, using dark magic to manipulate and control people." (Insert HUH? emoji here.) Looking back now, it's laughable how crazy this all was, but when it happened, I was so shocked, sad, and utterly bewildered. His accusations couldn't have been farther from the truth, so it was very confusing as to where he could come up with such blatant lies and then spit them out to his 10,000-plus followers as truth.

Over the next several days, the situation escalated as some of his followers private messaged me, accusing me of manipulating the masses with dark tactics. It was the craziest week of my life. I was being asked to defend and prove myself to a bunch of strangers on the internet. I went from confused, to angry, to wanting to get my lawyers involved for defamation. But nothing I said to him or his followers helped. They truly believed that self-help authors and people in the personal development industry are manipulators who have a dark agenda behind their messages. They were convinced that anyone with a large public following and blue Instagram check was part of a dark witch cult and had been trained to exploit and deceive people. Because there was no truth to these accusations, it may have seemed harmless, and I could have easily brushed it off, but the situation felt intense due to their adamant belief that I was someone I wasn't. No amount of reasoning would shift their perspective—their beliefs created their reality. No matter how much integrity and love I was in, it would never be seen as genuine because of their core belief that people cannot be trusted, especially if they are in the public eye. And this is why this lesson is important: our beliefs really do create our reality, and sometimes our beliefs can keep us from seeing the truth.

This is a classic example of how our views can harm us and others. We all have limiting beliefs, and most of us aren't aware how these beliefs are forming our reality. You may have heard of *cognitive dissonance*, a psychological concept that explains how we sometimes lie to ourselves to protect our version of reality. We each have beliefs and perspectives that are important to us and help shape our worldview, but when we are presented with new information that threatens or contradicts this original view, we try to ignore it or explain it away because it makes us uncomfortable. Your brain and ego try to avoid discomfort, so they will convince you that the new information is wrong or cannot fit within your current worldview—so instead of accepting the new information, you change your interpretation of the reality you've been presented with so it fits within your own beliefs.

It can be extremely uncomfortable to learn new things that contradict what we thought we knew. Our entire worldview can be rocked to its core when this happens. Learning that a loved one has been cheating on you when you thought your partnership was great, being diagnosed with a life-threatening disease when you believed you were taking excellent care of yourself, loving pizza but being told by your doctor that you're dairy and gluten intolerant—these are all examples of situations where two conflicting beliefs, values, or attitudes collide, causing various forms of discomfort and frustration.

The best thing we can do to start to implement the lesson that our beliefs create our reality is to first recognize that our beliefs are not always truth. They are opinions. Our beliefs can often block us from seeing the truth of many situations. In my situation, it became obvious that the social media trolls were stuck in their beliefs, and no amount of truth I presented would shift their perspective. But because I was far enough into my spiritual practice and had been teaching for over a decade on how to stay aligned with your true self, I decided to put my tools to the test. I remembered that when people attack you with criticism, it says nothing about you but is merely a reflection of them and their own projections. And since everything is a projection in this world, this means that criticism is merely an illusion that aims to separate you from knowing your true self.

LIFE TRUTH: ALL CRITICISM IS AN ILLUSION, AS IT'S A SEPARATION FROM LOVE.

When you know who you are and are aligned with Source Energy, criticism cannot harm you because you are connected to your true nature, the unshakable inner peace within. But even when you're fairly secure in this knowing, it can be hard to detach from critics. The first thing I did to detach from the drama was to ask myself key questions about the situation. The next time you are met with criticism or a belief someone else has about you, you can ask yourself these same questions.

1. Why did this person say what they are saying?

2. What is their belief (worldview) that is creating this reality for them?

3. Is there truth in what they are saying?

4. If there is no truth, then why am I angry?

5. Can I transform this situation with more love and forgiveness?

Lesson 153 in *A Course in Miracles* says, "In my defenselessness my safety lies." I knew that by defending myself, I would only cause more disharmony and make the situation worse. So I stopped engaging in the drama and instead turned my focus back to my own inner world. There was no truth in what was being said publicly about me, and because there was no truth, I decided there was no need for me to be upset or participate in their nonsense anymore. I didn't care what other people thought about me because I knew it wasn't real. I know myself, and I know God knows who I am. Ultimately, what other people say about us is not about us but about their own experience of life. In this release, I forgave the Instagram page owner for attacking me and lying about my character. I dropped my guard and sent him and his followers love and prayers, forgave them all, and then moved on. By releasing the situation, even though it wasn't resolved with that person in real time, I found peace in my heart.

This experience reminded me how much our beliefs can harm or help us. We can learn to disengage with our own limiting beliefs the same way we let go of the opinions of others, because all beliefs are opinion. To get to truth, we must go deeper into a place of intuition and knowing. Knowing is an unshakable awareness that what is—is. Opinions and beliefs can damage our ability to see truth because every person operates under a *confirmation bias*. This is the tendency to look for information that supports, rather than rejects, our preconceptions. Be honest for a second and think about your core beliefs and perspectives of the world. Where do your beliefs and opinions come from? Most of us feel that our convictions are rational, logical, impartial, and based on the result of years of experience. But in reality, our beliefs are not only shaped by those around us and our driving needs, but they are also often based on paying attention to the information that upholds them—while at the same time tending to ignore the information that challenges them. Perhaps the most important thing to realize is confirmation biases impact how we gather information, all while influencing how we interpret and recall information. For example, people who support or oppose a particular issue or party will not only seek information to support it, they will also interpret news stories in a way that upholds their existing ideas. At the same time, they will remember details in a way that reinforces these attitudes.

I saw this play out in my own family dynamics. A few years ago, my brother and I got into a heated discussion about current events. My brother believes the mainstream media is credible and always telling the truth, whereas I have developed a belief that most corporate-owned media in general cannot be trusted, since they are all owned by the same corporations and they manipulate details and headlines for ratings. As we were going back and forth trying to prove our cases to one another, my brother kept sending me more mainstream media articles on the topic. With every one he sent, I found holes and issues, mainly because I didn't trust those sources. But from my perspective (and my background in journalism and advertising), I had been trained to go deeper and see how things can be presented to persuade a reader into thinking a specific way. I pointed this out to him and sent independent journalists' articles instead, but he disregarded them as not credible.

I finally said, "Because our beliefs are fundamentally different views and opinions, we won't arrive at the same place on this issue, which is okay. We will just keep going in circles because what we focus on will always be through the lens of our own opinions." As I was explaining this to him, I found myself feeling more aggravated and defensive. He paused and said, "My love for you and our bond is infinitely stronger than anything we ever discuss." When he said that, a wave of calm rushed over me, and I not only felt safe to express my feelings, but also felt that I was seen through the filter of my brother's love. He brought up the point that even though our beliefs are different, it doesn't have to separate us. It could bring us closer together if we allow for it. And isn't this what we all want from one another, to be seen and feel safe to express ourselves without judgment or shame? Even if someone has a different belief system, it doesn't make them wrong, for they are aligning with a perspective that meets their soul's current needs. If we can all apply a more compassionate, loving response to others, then when we disagree, we will see that our beliefs are not fact, nor do they define us—and what matters most is our connection to others.

I personally witnessed the life-changing power of shifting our beliefs during the 2020 election year, which felt more emotionally charged than any year prior. During that time, I began to look at my own beliefs and biases and decided to challenge them. I was open to watching new things and listening to new ideas, and I questioned everything that was presented on all media. I followed friends and accounts of people who had different beliefs from mine in an effort to learn and listen. I banished my all-or-nothing thinking about what was the right or wrong way to do things, and I accepted and allowed for all beliefs. In opening up my worldview, I learned so much about others and grew my own compassion as well. And you'll never believe how much my strict, hard, fast beliefs that once were nonnegotiable loosened their grip. I was open to hearing others' opinions and ideas and open to seeing all people's perspectives, even if I didn't agree with them.

By being willing to go past my own beliefs and accept new possibilities and ways of being, my world became more compassionate, expansive, and peaceful. It became clear to me that people have beliefs that serve them where they are on their journey of life, and that their truth is real and valid for them. Who am I to tell them what to believe or that they are wrong because it is different from what I believe? We can all coexist, differences and all. What each one of us is craving is a recognition of self. When you can hold space for another and their beliefs even if they are different, you show maturity, respect, and love. As I started to practice this compassion, I had more respect for others, which is important because we all want to be seen, acknowledged, and heard.

LIFE TRUTH: ACKNOWLEDGMENT EQUALS LOVE. WHEN YOU ALLOW OTHERS AND YOURSELF TO BE SEEN, YOU ARE LOVE IN ACTION.

If you are feeling stuck in the drama of criticism or stubborn beliefs and want to break free, this prayer can help guide you forward.

A Prayer for Peace

I detach from anything that seeks to separate.

Anything that says, "Us versus them."

Anything that says, "My way or the highway."

Anything that seeks to destroy, condemn, shame, or blame.

Instead, I choose unity.

I choose kindness, compassion.

I choose love.

Have you ever wondered why some people thrive in some situations while others fail? When the world at large or our own personal world falls into a crisis, there are those who fall down with it, and there are those who rise and lift themselves up into more success, despite the most difficult circumstances. It all comes back to our beliefs. If you believe you are destined for doom and you are at the mercy of the world's circumstances, then that will be your experience. You will attract situations to reinforce your core beliefs. On the other hand, if you believe you live in a loving, abundant, dynamic Universe and that your actions matter, you can create a more rewarding life—no matter what your past is or what you've been through and no matter what is happening outside of you—and your outcome will be very different.

The other day I was catching up with an old friend, Lewis, whom I hadn't connected with since high school (over twenty years ago). As we were catching up, we started to share how our lives had unfolded. He told me the reason he had never married and didn't have kids at age forty was because of the way he had grown up. He said his parents never showed him any love, nor did they teach him how to believe in himself. I listened to his story and couldn't help but see how this was a limiting belief. I said to him, "Is it possible that's a story you're telling yourself? Because I grew up in a loving household and a very positive environment and my parents supported me, yet I am not married, nor do I have kids at age forty. If your reasoning were true, that would mean I would be married with children by now, right?" He said, "I never thought of it that way," and we discussed that maybe the reason he was single was because he hadn't met the person he truly wanted to be with. Maybe it is about Divine Timing and the bigger life plan. Maybe he didn't want to settle. He laughed and said, "Well, yeah, that is true. I haven't actually met anyone I really want to settle down with." In that moment, he rewrote his story and let go of the limitation he was putting onto himself.

We don't have to blame our past for our present circumstances. Many of us blame ourselves and make it our own fault for not being where we think we should be. These are limitations, and they block us from living a connected, fulfilled life. A limiting belief such as "My family background limits what I can become in life" can turn into an empowering belief: "My past does not create my future. I can become anything I want to when I believe in myself." Or something like "I need more resources, time, money, etc., in order to be happy, do what I love, start my own business, etc.," with a little mindset shift can turn into an empowering perspective: "I always have enough time, money, and energy for what is most important to me." We can always retrain our brain to focus on the better. The goal is to have beliefs that empower us rather than hinder us.

We do not see things as they are, we see them as we are.

ANAÏS NIN

On a personal level, what do you believe about yourself? Our own view of our selves is the most important focus we can have. If you appreciate yourself and practice self-love and see your worth, your life is incredibly different than if you live through a lens of feeling unworthy, ugly, and ashamed. We will create our reality based on the beliefs and projections that we constantly focus on. Abraham and Esther Hicks say, "What you are living is the evidence of what you are thinking and feeling—every single time."

I have a friend who is a prolific author. Every time she releases a book, it hits the *New York Times* Best Seller list, which is unheard of for many authors. I asked her what her success secret is, and without taking a breath, she responded, "I believe in myself!" The more I thought about it, the more it made sense, since each book project—from prepublish, to launch, to after the book came out—was full of a no-fail attitude. Confidence is attractive. Believing in yourself and your worth is a powerful attractor. It will extend into everything you do. With my friend, this energy is transferred into the entire marketing and release of her books. When you believe and trust in yourself, you are unstoppable.

LIFE TRUTH: WE BECOME WHAT WE THINK ABOUT MOST, AND THE UNIVERSE CONSTANTLY REARRANGES ITSELF TO ACCOMMODATE AND ALIGN WITH OUR VERSION OF REALITY.

So if you don't like an aspect of the life that you are living, ask yourself what your belief about this situation is. And then, shift that belief. When you do, you can and will radically shift your results. Do your beliefs help you feel good? Do they bring you peace? This is what we want to ask ourselves, because if your beliefs are harming yourself or others or causing separation, then they are beliefs that are rooted in fear. Aligning your beliefs with love is the way to peace. Lesson 75 from *A Course in Miracles* says, "You are at peace, and you bring peace wherever you go." This means we, in our natural state, are peaceful, loving beings, but our beliefs and perceptions can often rob us of this connection. Align your beliefs with truth and love for the ultimate freedom.

Inner peace is a choice we make daily, moment by moment. It is easier to do when we believe in something bigger than ourselves. The more intention you put into your faith, the more freedom you will feel. In this freedom, you feel certainty—a pure, inner confidence that shines through all your actions.

We can gauge our peace based on connection to the universal Source Energy. I believe in spirit guides and universal helpers. I believe we live in a loving Universe and that this love is within us and all around us always. Whenever I fall into a place of doubt or worry, I return to my faith. This faith is certainty, and it sets me free. By no means am I telling you what to believe in. The point here is that when you align with your truth, that is true faith, connecting to what is real and true for you. We all have to find beliefs that work for us and serve our soul's growth. No matter what your belief system is, it is important to have a connection to love. Some connect to it through religion, others through music or nature. Maybe you connect to the Universe when you are dancing, singing, or hiking. Or maybe you feel the love of God when you are supporting others through acts of service or charity, or giving your time, money, or energy to support causes you care about. We all have moments when we feel connected to our best self. These moments are a direct channel to the universal, loving Source Energy. If you currently hold any beliefs that are separating you from others or otherwise blocking you from accessing this unlimited stream of well-being, then it is time to renegotiate them.

The more you trust in your own spiritual faith, whatever and however that looks like to you, the easier your life will be. Things will flow more, and the outside world will affect you less. You will no longer be rocked off center when people try to derail you with criticism or when attack thoughts surface from yourself or others. You will stand firm in your truth and believe in the power of the love within you and all around you. This is your superpower. With this constant connection, you become an example to others.

When you move past your own opinions and beliefs, you arrive at a deeper place of knowing. Your knowing is your truth and your connection to the Universe. When you are committed to this connection and confident in your own faith, you change your mind about the world. You no longer need the world to fit your own perspective or preferences, but rather you relax into an inner awareness that all is as it should be. You no longer feel the need to get others to see the world the way you do because you trust and focus on your inner wisdom.

Your inner knowing will align you with what is real. It can turn conflict into opportunity and trauma into purpose and healing. When you commit to staying open and being willing to see things in a new way, you put yourself on a personal growth trajectory. You say to the Universe, "I am open and willing to expand." In your expansive state, you will always be rewarded. You will experience joy, love, abundance, and an unshakable inner peace. Release your view of the world that you thought you knew, and embrace all perspectives with an open heart and mind.

Let's put this lesson into practice:

We all have beliefs that shape our reality, but when we use discernment to see if those beliefs are hurting or helping us, it's the first step to clearing out the harmful ones for good. We can do this by detaching from drama. To apply this lesson, Your Beliefs Create Your Reality, try these steps.

Step 1: Take a mental inventory.
Look at your experiences and life situations, and take stock of each of them. Which people, places, beliefs, habits, and situations are supporting you and your growth, and which ones are limiting you? Get honest about the situations in your life that are not going as well as

you'd hoped. Then ask, "What are my beliefs about this situation?" Recognize which thoughts are limiting you. You have the opportunity now to let go of everything holding you back. Even if you are not aware of all the things blocking you, you can set the intention to release them so you can begin to step into your power. Lesson 281 in *A Course in Miracles* says, "I can be hurt by nothing but my thoughts." The beliefs you have about yourself and the world are important, as they direct your outcomes. Work on aligning all your beliefs to love so you feel empowered and purpose driven.

Step 2: Detach with dignity.
Abraham Hicks says, "The secret of the Universe really is minding your own business. What we mean by that is, don't get so involved in the desires or beliefs of others that you cause confusion or chatter in your own vibration and compromise your own alignment." When you remove yourself physically and emotionally from criticism and drama, you can gain a more truthful perspective on the situation. When you are in the midst of frustrating experiences, it's like being trapped inside a tornado—you can't see things clearly. But setting yourself apart from the experience will give you a bird's-eye view of the whole situation. As you gain more clarity, you start to see what is worth your time and attention and what is not. Always align your attention with what feels good and peaceful. Be willing to have boundaries and detach with your dignity intact, and focus on experiences that are true and in integrity with you. This does not mean you are naïve or blind to what is happening in the world; it simply means you energetically align with yourself first so you can be of higher service to the world and come to each situation with more clarity, purpose, and love.

Step 3: Grow past what you know.
Kimberly Carter Gamble, the producer and director of the movies *Thrive* and *Thrive II,* shared a story about her grandmother, who lived a long, healthy, and happy life to the age of 103. Her grandmother believed that the success of her life and making it through such challenging times in history were because of her ability to try on an idea. She said, "You have to be able to try on an idea like an outfit. You don't have to like it, you can even return

it, but at least you try it on."[15] If we all commit to listening to one another with compassion and an open heart, we can come together in our humanity and unite with more love. This requires a personal responsibility to commit to going beyond what we already know. Be open to learning more, and question your own beliefs often. To grow, we must push to new levels of awareness. One of the most important tools we have is critical thinking. If we can be more open-minded and willing to look beyond what we already know, our world can shift. This requires an ability to suspend disbelief and temporarily hold conflicting views long enough to see if the new perspective feels right. When we can do this, the truth will always be revealed, and freedom prevails.

Step 4: Select sovereign solutions.

With its conflicting information and constant push-pull dynamic, the outside world often works overtime to take our attention away from what matters most. Your inner world is your connection to truth, to the Source, to love. Don't fall into the traps of taking sides or pushing against what you fear. As Maureen J. St. Germain, the author of *Waking Up in 5D: A Practical Guide to Multidimensional Transformation*, says, "Any time we participate in mass consciousness culture we are giving our permission to everything that holds us back." What does this mean? There are energy levels to everything, and most of what we see out in the world is blame, fear, shame, and disharmony. Yet your sovereign self is where your true power lies. Our true nature craves community, collaboration, love, and compassion. In essence, we go against our true selves by participating in the mass manipulations. When you put your attention into something, you fuel it and subscribe energetically to its emotional charge. Now, this isn't about being apathetic or ignoring current events. Instead, it's about aligning with your sovereign self, staying in your power, and connecting to your inner light first—because from this place, you have clarity, discernment, and purpose. You can then make choices from your true nature rather than from fear.

---

15   *Thrive II: This Is What It Takes*, directed by Kimberly Carter Gamble, written by Mary Earle Chase, Foster Gamble, Kimberly Carter Gamble, and Neal Rogin, released September 26, 2020, 151 minutes, thriveon.com/thrive-ii-this-is-what-it-takes/.

Step 5: Make peace your priority so negativity cannot exist.
In all situations, we have an option to see the dark or the light, to embrace fear or walk in love. Peace lives in every moment when you make it a priority. You may be stuck in fear, but fear breeds fear, which means every choice you make in fear will give you even more fear. Instead, relinquish your control and let love in. Inviting light to all situations will help uplift you and bring you harmony.

If there is a situation in your life you are overthinking or worrying about, look instead at the light within it. Because Source Energy and love are in all things, everything is an expression of the Creator. Seeking to see this truth will bring you more peace and will help ground out any negative charge around the situation. When you realize the Divine is in all things, you see that you don't have to make anything happen. You just allow. See this time in your life as an opportunity to awaken to the truth of who you are. Dive into your awakening—the decision to think and act from love rather than fear is the catalyst to true inner peace.

Questions to ask:

1. Which people, places, beliefs, habits, and situations are supporting me and my growth, and which ones are limiting?

2. How can I detach from drama and align with my inner light?

3. What belief, pattern, or habit is no longer serving me?

Our beliefs are powerful shapers of the world we perceive. When we look at any limitations and discord in our life, we can look at the belief that is the source of this continuing pattern. When we shift out of these beliefs, we radically transform our life. In the next lesson, we will learn how important it is to respect others on their own life journey and show up more fully on our own path to align with our true nature. You'll discover how relationships play an intricate role in your life lessons and how to let go of energetic strains when it comes to other people.

LESSON 5

EVERYONE IS ON THEIR OWN JOURNEY

A few years ago, I went to Bali, Indonesia, for the first time and discovered a new activity that quickly became one of my favorite experiences: ecstatic dance. Ecstatic dance is a form of dance in which you let loose completely and dive fully into the moment, surrendering yourself to the rhythm as you let the music take you wherever you need to go. From an outside perspective, it may look like a bunch of people have lost their minds, undulating their bodies to mimic the sound of the music and moving in all kinds of strange ways, but when you are fully in it, it's the ultimate form of creative self-expression. When done with full abandon, what results is a complete liberation from judgment, shame, and even self-sabotage. Hello, pure freedom! When I did it for the first time in Bali, in a yoga barn with hundreds of other people from all around the world, something miraculous happened. I saw how everyone is on their own journey.

I was with some friends, and one seemed scared to let loose. She was so worried about what others would think about her. For the entire hour, she was watching how others responded to her. But what she didn't realize was that everyone was far more engrossed in their own experience than worrying about or focusing on her. My other friend was quite the opposite in her approach; she stripped off all her clothes and danced in her bikini, proud of her body and fully embracing the flow while literally running circles around everyone. She was in her fullest expression, as if to say, "Nothing can hold me back. Here I am, world." And then there was me, somewhere in the middle of the two of them. I gave it my all until I could no longer breathe. I had bursts of incredible highs, and then moments of reprieve while sitting it out on the side, catching my breath and preparing for the next round.

While I was resting and taking an active recovery from my sweat session (aka pure euphoria topped with utopian bliss), it occurred to me how much this experience was a metaphor for life. The live DJ played the music, and we all moved our bodies in any way we felt was needed. Everyone was interpreting the music differently. Some people were doing yoga poses while some did back bends; some were breakdancing while others were busting out pop moves; and still others danced together in unison, connected as one. Some were sitting in the corner; others were lying down in the middle of it all. There we were, all together, yet each in our own mini universe. The experience reflected how we are all in a dance in life, during which we come together and fall apart. The true lesson revealed is that we are all on our own journey.

This lesson plays out the most in our relationships. I used to have a best friend, and we would talk sometimes two or three times a day. We met up weekly for brunch and coffee dates. It was amazing to have that type of connection with someone, a true soul sister. But over time, our relationship changed. At first, I kept trying to hold on to the old version of us, but our lives were pulling us in different directions. When we made plans, she would cancel at the last minute—something she would never have done before. She said she would call or text, but weeks turned into months, and I never heard from her. Whenever I did try to plan or reach out, it was a strained effort. Eventually my trust and faith in her completely disappeared as she made promises but never followed through. I kept trying to figure out what had happened to cause such distance. Was it something I said or did? Maybe she was mad at me. Isn't that typical? We often worry and blame ourselves when things change in relationships. But this habit of thinking I was the problem had to end.

After several months of her canceling on me, I finally spoke up and said how I was feeling. I told her that I missed us and felt distant, and that to grow and maintain our friendship there had to be two-way effort. I shared that I felt hurt when she continued to blow me off and that her actions made me feel like I didn't matter to her. As you can imagine, it turned into an argument. She started to defend herself and said she was busy and didn't have the luxury of hanging out because of her daily demands and responsibilities. After hearing her response, it occurred to me how I was making it all about me, but her situation was about her. It became obvious each one of us had a totally different perspective on the situation. Often, we think it is about us, but it never is.

LIFE TRUTH: WHEN WE LOOK AT OTHERS' ACTIONS AS A MIRROR, WE CAN DISCOVER WHAT THEIR BEHAVIOR TELLS US ABOUT US.

I looked at her actions of ignoring, canceling, and not making time for me, and how this had made me push harder to get what I wanted and over-give my time and energy. I saw how this was a pattern in my life. Her actions made me feel disrespected and unloved, but her actions had nothing to do with me. We often make a situation worse by interpreting through the filter of our own insecurities. This just so happened to be a pattern of mine. I would often over-give and sacrifice myself in order to be liked, accepted, or acknowledged. I call this the autopilot reaction. We all have autopilot reactions when things happen and we don't get what we need, so we overcompensate and outsource our unhealed pain by projecting onto others what we want them to do. For me, my pain was not feeling supported and respected. When we encounter these situations, we revert to a behavior that started in childhood in order to protect ourselves and get us what we needed most back then. For me, this was over-giving in order to be liked. I was over-giving of my energy and efforts for my friend who was too busy for me, and this brought up my unhealed childhood wounds.

When I was little, we moved around a lot, and with each new school came a new group of kids who often made fun of me. My parents both worked long hours at new jobs, which led me to believe as a child that they didn't have time for me and that my needs didn't matter. I never felt like others were sincere or cared about me, so to get my need for belonging met, I became a people pleaser, often doing extra credit, staying after school to help the teacher clean up, etc. I would feel accepted and acknowledged for my efforts when the teacher appreciated me, which turned into me being called teacher's pet, so the cycle continued. Flash-forward to my adult life, where this unhealed wound of not feeling accepted by my peers was rearing its ferocious head. Through my argument with my friend, I realized that my frustration with her pulling away actually had nothing to do with her at all, but was connected to the deep-seated, unhealed wound that was opening through her actions. By her not staying consistent in our friendship, I was reminded of my inconsistent childhood of moving around and not having a solid set of friends. It exposed my insecurities and unpleasant childhood experiences of not being liked or feeling like I mattered.

Lessons 5 and 6 in *A Course in Miracles* say, "I am never upset for the reason I think . . . I am upset because I see something that is not there." So often, we react to situations in the present while not realizing that the current situation has nothing to do with the reason we are upset; rather, it's a situation from the past that is causing us disharmony. Most of us look outside of ourselves and want the outside world to change: "If only my fiancé would do the things I liked," or "If only my best friend told me how proud she is of me," or "If only my son would call me more." The list goes on with the secret demands we place on others, hoping they will change. And when and if they do, then we believe we will be okay and happiness will come.

Many of us feel stuck, trapped by circumstances, frustrated, and like we aren't where we are supposed to be. We feel as if something is missing. That *something missing* is often because we are projecting our needs and wants onto others. But this is once again an ego mastermind trick, trying to pull you away from your own soul's growth journey. Every single one of us has our own unique perspective, point of view, reason for being, and ultimately our own lesson that our soul needs for our greatest awakening potential. We come together with others on our soul journey to help mirror and support our own path.

When we look at our relationships as assignments, we can dive deeper into our own journey of life. With my friend, it was clear we had drifted apart and I was trying to hold on to something she was okay with releasing. I desperately grasped at trying to keep the old us together. But the old us couldn't exist anymore because both of us had changed so much. For many weeks, I was angry at her for letting our friendship go and seeing me as disposable, especially after how close we had been. Then I remembered the passage from *A Course in Miracles* that states, "If you attack error in another, you will hurt yourself." I learned that the anger I felt was just unprocessed sadness. I was being asked to let go of someone who meant a lot to me in my life. When we punish, push against, argue with, or withdraw from others in an effort to try to make them do what we want, this just strengthens their own resistance, because it is energetically felt and that negative energy pushes them away even more. It seemed the harder I tried to make our friendship work, the farther away my friend pulled. We can't make others change, but we can focus on our own behavior. The lesson in the moment for me was to turn my anger into compassion. I did this by putting myself in her shoes and trying to see things from her perspective.

We can shift our own beliefs and patterns surrounding our relationships by adopting the concept of *radical compassion*. Tara Brach, the author of the book *Radical Compassion*, says the term *radical compassion* means including the vulnerability of this life—all life—in our hearts. Radical compassion is rooted in mindful, embodied presence, and it is expressed actively through caring that includes all beings.[16] When we make choices inspired from a place of

---

16   Tara Brach, *Radical Compassion: Learning to Love Yourself and Your World with the Practice of RAIN* (New York: Penguin Life, 2020).

compassion versus our insecurities, we can be curious about others and nurture our connections with more love. Ultimately, living with compassion as a focus can give us insight into a bigger picture.

To me, radical compassion meant looking at things from a new perspective. I put myself in my friend's shoes and recognized that she was going through a lot. She was a recently divorced single mother with a full-time job, a small business on the side, and a teenage son in high school. She was prioritizing work and family (as she should), and in that moment, I saw that it was never about me. Her lifestyle had changed, and with that came new responsibilities for her. None of her not being able to make time for me was about me. It was about her just trying to make it through life. Most of the time when we are angry, it is because we are hurting inside. We are trying to hold on to a situation or person who we feel has wronged us, but really, we are just sad things didn't turn out differently.

When we understand that everyone has their own path to follow, we can see that nothing is about us. We don't have to take anything personally. Instead of thinking a situation is about us, we can put ourselves in other people's shoes and try to increase our compassion and awareness. I asked myself, "What would love do? How would love show up for this situation?" Love would be compassionate and kind to my friend and would recognize that her avoiding me was not about me. With this new awareness, I released the relationship and the stress I was putting on us. I prayed for her and sent her love, all while letting her know I would be there for her if and when she needed. But most importantly, I released my expectations of what I thought the relationship should be. I was trying so hard to hold on to what the Universe wanted me to release; the friendship had run its course.

We have the power to create optimal relationships, but we must first release all those that no longer align with our higher selves. After parting ways and releasing the relationship energetically, I sat down and created a list of what I need and want in a friendship. I wrote, "I am looking for like-minded people who enjoy personal growth. I want friends who want to prioritize friendships and grow our connection." After writing my desires down, within one week of my declaring to the Universe what I wanted in a friendship, I was invited to an author mastermind group with amazing women who inspire, motivate, and uplift me. Over the years, our mastermind group has turned into deep, rewarding friendships and a beautiful sisterhood that is so much stronger than what I was trying to hold on to with people from my past.

When we let go, we grow. All of us are on a spiritual growth path and always moving forward. Sometimes we progress in new directions, away from those who led us to where we currently are. This is normal. But the clearer you are about what you want in relationships, the easier it will be for the Universe to bring it to you, and for you to release what is no longer aligned.

LIFE TRUTH: ALL RELATIONSHIPS ARE DIVINE ASSIGNMENTS.

Sarah Armide, an intuitive reader and YouTuber, says, "Life is the workshop, and you and your higher self have a contract to purify all of the distortions within you."[17] Every single one of us is on our own journey. We each have our own individual lessons, which means that the experiences in which we participate will be different. We can't compare ourselves to anyone because we truly are all unique and on our own path. I used to compare myself to other authors, only to realize that their soul lessons were completely different from mine. So naturally, their career path was different from mine because my own soul had its own path to explore, as did theirs. Recognizing this can free us from the frustration of thinking life needs to look a certain way.

If you find yourself looking to others, comparing yourself, or needing others to fix your situation—whether it be wanting them to do or say

---

17   Sarah Armide, "Separation, Discrimination, Trauma & The Ascension," YouTube video, youtube.com /watch?v=EWW7FVCwnhQ&t=319s.

certain things or behave in a certain way—you have unknowingly but actively participated in giving your power away. Marianne Williamson said, "Relationships are the Holy Spirit's laboratories in which He brings together people who have the maximal opportunity for mutual growth."[18] And this concept of all relationships being Divine Assignments is based on teachings in almost all spiritual texts.

> Everyone is on a different journey, but truly on
> the same path: the one which is of love.

DR. JAMES MARTIN PEEBLES

When you really sit down to think about it, we are always in multiple relationships and experiencing different frequencies and dimensions of love: in our relationships with various friends, co-workers, nature, life, neighbors, family, our bodies, food, etc. But the most important partnership is the one with Source Energy and ourselves. To be alive is to be in a relationship with life. Our mission is to increase communication with all of it in order to grow into more love and compassion.

Many relationships will end, but not all assignments end. Some last for lifetimes. The main point is to recognize that every person on the planet is on their own soul adventure, and we come together and dance through life. But ultimately each person's life and path is about them, as yours is about you. And this is not selfish but self-fulfilling, as it is the law of the Universe that all souls are designed to grow. Through our relationships, we can learn the lessons and take the "life" tests. We are like magnets— attracting, reflecting, and rejecting what is not in alignment. Sometimes it is in our highest good to release a relationship. If you need to release a person from your life, it doesn't have to create a huge, dramatic fallout. When you walk the path of your true self, you will end things with peace and love, for you no longer entertain a desire for dramatic situations.

---

18   Marianne Williamson, *A Return to Love: Reflections on the Principles of A Course in Miracles* (New York: HarperOne, 1996).

Take these steps when releasing a relationship or changing its form:

Step 1: Ask, "Will changing this relationship improve my inner peace?"

Step 2: Ask the Universe for support to receive the inner strength and courage to change the form of the relationship if need be. And have the strength to change what you cannot accept.

Step 3: Be willing to release the relationship with love. You can repeat the mantra "I am willing to release this relationship with peace and harmony."

In her book *Soul Love: Awakening Your Heart Centers*, Sanaya Roman reminds us that "When releasing a relationship, you don't need a reason to release it. You don't have to overthink it; this is an opportunity for you to trust yourself."[19] Feel your feelings and let them guide you. You know how you feel around people. Does the relationship cause stress, worry, and angst? If so, pay close attention to these signals as they may be affecting your well-being.

Releasing Relationships Meditation
(For When Things Just Feel Off)

If you want to leave or change a relationship, you can work on a
soul level to ensure both of you go in peace, love, and harmony.
Close your eyes and imagine the person standing next to you.
Imagine that you have both been walking along a path
together and now the path is dividing. There is a fork in the road.
It is in your highest good for both of you
to go forth on your separate paths.
Know that each of you has become more of who
you are supposed to be and must now concentrate on
this new route for optimal growth and awareness.
Pay attention to how you feel in this moment of

---

19 Sanaya Roman, *Soul Love: Awakening Your Heart Centers* (Tiburon, CA: H J Kramer, 1997).

parting. Get in touch with your true feelings.
Trust the process and release this person with love.
It is necessary for you to grow and evolve past each other
in different directions for you to each get what you need.
There is no need to see this as an ending, but
rather focus on the new beginning.
See the relationship as a success. Reflect on all the experiences
you created together. Celebrate the relationship with love.
Be willing to release the other person and
allow each other to go your own way.
Send them love and repeat the mantra "I thank you
for our relationship. I release you with love."

* This meditation and concept are inspired by *Soul Love: Awaken Your Heart Centers* by Sanaya Roman.

As you learn your lessons, you will advance on your soul journey. Sanaya Roman says, "If someone is leaving you or has recently left, is pulling away or acting indifferent, do not dwell on what you could say or do to draw this person closer. Instead reflect on how this person's actions are mirroring something that is going on within you. Ask, how have you been leaving this relationship yourself? Perhaps you've been distant or questioning the relationship yourself." Whether it is a romantic partner, a sibling, a friend, or even someone you have recently met, all of our relationships present grand opportunities for us to grow and learn more about our true selves. We don't always realize it, but we often put extra burdens on others and ourselves when we idolize and look up to others and put them on pedestals. Looking up to people and seeing them as better than us keeps us from feeling our true worth.

For the first few years of my career as a writer, I looked up to Elizabeth Gilbert. Well—to say I looked up to her is actually a massive understatement, as I had her on a pedestal so high that you'd get vertigo trying to get to her. I read *Eat Pray Love* when I was diagnosed with depression, and that book and her writing style inspired me to follow my inner voice to leave what wasn't working, travel the world, and become a published author. She became my shining example of what is possible when you decide you are worth it and leave the trappings of society behind to follow your authentic self and blaze your own path forward.

For years I followed her career and read every new article or blog she put out. I hung on to her every word like gold. She unknowingly became my she-ro and my all-knowing wise sage, nudging me forward. In one of my Facebook posts, I quoted and tagged her, and when she liked the post, I about died. My whole world felt complete—my idol had acknowledged me! (Take that, childhood bullies. I *am* somebody after all.) I didn't know it at the time, but my mild (okay, well, *wild*) obsession with another person was taking away my own connection with myself, and it was distracting me from honing my own craft. I wanted so much to be like Elizabeth Gilbert and have her acknowledge me that I was losing my own voice.

She came to Portland, Oregon, for one of her book tours, and I made sure to go. In my mind, this was my chance for us to finally meet. I would hand her my first published book, and that would be my ticket for her to endorse it. I was sure that soon after, she'd call her pal Oprah, and soon enough, the three of us would all be drinking passionfruit iced tea in Oprah's backyard rose garden as we toasted to this fantastic life and our newfound friendship. Many of us do similar things without thinking much about it. We fantasize about best-case scenarios involving other people, or we look up to others and assume they have it all together, and we believe that by positioning ourselves alongside others who have it more together, we somehow will become more complete. But when we place our attention outside of ourselves and focus it on others, we are misdirecting our own light. We are making them gods and putting all our faith and focus into them instead of the true Creator. As *A Course in Miracles* teaches, "Idols are but a substitute for your reality. In some way you believe they will complete your little self, offer safety in a world perceived as dangerous. An idol is a false impression or false belief that constitutes a gap between the divine source energy and the world we see."

LIFE TRUTH: THE WORLD OF IDOLS IS A DISTRACTION, AS ITS PURPOSE IS TO SEPARATE US FROM ONE ANOTHER AND KEEP US IN THE ILLUSION OF HIERARCHY.

Whether someone is an author, an A-list actor, a famous sports star, a politician, a romantic partner, or a best friend, no one is better than you. The wounded part of us, the inner child that still needs nurturing, will overshadow our own needs by projecting outward to focus on the greatness of others, believing that they will save us. When we recognize that everyone is equal and there is no hierarchy, we can balance ourselves in more light. This can be challenging because we live in a world that strives to push us into always craving more. More success, more beauty, more money, more power, more likes—yet none of this matters to the soul's individual journey. So often we look to leaders, politicians, gurus, teachers, and celebrities for the answers. But they are just people trying to figure it out, too. As long as you are a human being, you will go through stuff. People we look up to are not exempt from the deep, rich learning of life; they may just be better at hiding it when they stumble.

Take your attention off others and return to you. You know you best, and your insights come from your own experience. When we idolize anyone, we forget that their journey is not the same as ours, and even the most well-put-together and well-intentioned person is still going through their own life lessons and personal stuff. The "stuff" being the soul lessons and the spiritual growth that we are all destined for.

While I was at Elizabeth Gilbert's book tour event, I found myself growing more and more disgruntled. I felt let down after learning that there was no opportunity to meet her in person, which led me to only be half-engaged with the rest of the event, so the talk she gave didn't feel inspiring. There were more than a thousand people in the audience, and I was in the nosebleed seats—so far away that she looked like a speck onstage. As I festered in my frustration, it became clear to me that I had put such grandiose expectations on this evening and on her that when I actually saw her in person and heard her speak, I thought to myself, "Is this it?"

Then she shared something in her talk that hit me smack in the face. She told a story about meeting one of the people she admired most and said, "I recommend never meeting your idols, because you quickly realize they are just as messed up as you, and we are all just doing the best we can." I had to smile to myself—the Universe was reminding me that all relationships are assignments, even the ones we have with people we admire. It seemed like she was there to deliver the message I needed to hear to free me from my illusions of separation and lack of self-worth. I made a promise to myself that day to never idolize or look up to anyone else ever again, for we are all equal and all have different lessons to learn. I realized no one is better than or less than, and we are all just traveling together on this earth, doing the best we can. Of course, it is wonderful to have people we respect and look to as teachers and guides, and it is great to have coaches or mentors, but we must first realize that our internal guide and our connection to Source is where our true power lives. No one knows you better than you do. Idolizing people only causes discord with each other and within our selves.

LIFE TRUTH: THERE IS FREEDOM IN LETTING ALL THINGS BE IN THEIR OWN TIME AND PLACE, STARTING WITH YOURSELF.[20]

It's helpful to understand that all relationships have a purpose, and some run their course. Remember that while everyone is on their own journey in life, we come together to share in each other's adventure. You can't change others, so relax more into the journey of life, and enjoy your own life creation. Be kind and gentle with yourself. You are doing an amazing job on your journey. Take comfort in releasing all judgment, comparison, shame, or blame, for everyone is always on their own path.

---

20   Modified from Dr. James Martin Peebles through Summer Bacon, "The Three Principles," accessed September 8, 2020, summerbacon.com/the-three-principles.html.

Let's put this lesson into practice:

To implement this lesson, Everyone Is on Their Own Journey, try these steps.

Step 1: Recognize everyone is on their own journey.
We are all here on Earth as spiritual renegades at the courageous forefront of cosmic reality, on a mission to advance into a greater understanding of love. What we do with our time on Earth is completely up to us, but choosing to live with intention, well-being, hope, and joy is the shortcut to happiness. Take the pressure off yourself and others to react or be a certain way and instead honor them on their own path of personal self-discovery.

Step 2: Dive deeper into your own life dance.
When you take a step back and see that everyone is experiencing life in their own personal way, you start to see everything as a dance in which you co-create with others, and your relationships become Divine Assignments and experiments. Life itself becomes more fluid, and you understand that you get to create your own reality. You soon want to make your choices from love and in connection to Source because this is your true self. When you focus on others and need them to do what you want, however, you cut yourself off from this divinity. Your mission is to courageously accept the challenge to rise above the illusion of believing you're not good enough and to be the light by honoring your own path. In doing this, you respect others on their journey, and you stop taking things personally because everyone is always doing the best they can with where they are on their own soul's growth adventure. We are here to expand into our potential and be a reflection for others as they are for us.

Step 3: Trust that everyone is playing their part.
Start to see the whole world as a giant movie screen or play and that you are witnessing the story unfolding. Much like watching entertainment, you don't always get emotionally involved as you witness the characters exploring their own journey because there is a separation between the

character and yourself. This allowance is the same energy we can apply to our own life. When friends or family come to you and express their opinions and desires, you can watch them as you would characters in a movie and trust that they have their own plot twists to explore. You are part of their narrative, but you don't have to get entangled, emotional, or involved. The same is true for the events occurring out in the world. You can witness them without emotional entanglement (unless, of course, you want to get involved—again, it is always about alignment and what feels good for you). Trust that everyone is playing their part in the story and adventure of our lives. Instead of comparing yourself to others, or getting involved in their dramas, or focusing on something that has nothing to do with you, you can focus on your own story and the narrative that you want to live. Be the hero of your own grand adventure.

Questions to ask:

1. How can I release all judgment, comparison, and shame and focus more on my own path?

2. Can I give myself more credit for all of the amazing things I've done?

3. How can I be more kind, compassionate, and loving to myself and others?

4. Which relationships feel strained, and which ones need more attention and care?

Now that we fully understand that everyone has their own life lessons and journey to embark on, we can see that our own life path is a special one and we are all interconnected. In the next lesson, you'll discover the four seasons of awakening to your true self and advancement for your soul, and how to release old paradigms so you can gracefully step into your new, emerging energy and navigate all changes with clarity and ease. Let's keep going.

LESSON 6

YOUR SOUL HAS SEASONS

nstead of struggling, resisting, and pushing so hard to move forward, re-lax; there is a much easier way. That's what my inner voice said in meditation one morning. At that point in my life, I was not a regular meditator. I didn't have time to do it, plus I was never able to reach the benefits that so many boasted about. People I knew who meditated regularly seemed to have this zen glow, which only frustrated me more because I couldn't understand how they achieved it. Meditating for me was like trying to get a seven-year-old to calm down on their birthday after eating cake and cookies and opening presents—impossible.

But during the phase of my life when anxiety was at its height, I was forced into meditation by sheer life circumstances. Sitting silently in a chair with my eyes closed seemed to be the only thing I could do that gave me a sense of relief. It was the *only* thing actually working in my life. I felt stuck in all other areas, and most of the things that used to flow and bring me immense joy suddenly came to a standstill and lacked the same fulfillment. I had been running a successful coaching practice and speaking business for almost a decade. But suddenly, several pieces of it came to a halt. The place where I grew up and had lived for decades, I no longer felt a connection to. Many friendships, upon deeper reflection, felt superficial and inauthentic. To top it all off, my health wasn't as strong as I had hoped, and naturally, I fell into a depression. It was as if everything I knew had been turned upside down and was falling apart. I kept asking, "Why is this happening? What is the lesson?" But as long as I was only asking *why*, I couldn't get to the *what*. The *what* was that it was all a blessing in disguise, as I was actually entering a new season of my soul.

When we are trapped in fear, stuck in transition, or lack clarity and confidence because of the unknown, feeling better requires a deeper sense of awareness of the rhythms of life and your soul's unique journey. I call these rhythms the *seasons of your soul*, which invites an awareness of your current situation and how it relates to the bigger picture of your life. I realized I was in the rest season of my soul, so pushing to try to make things happen wasn't going to change anything. It was time for me to relax, recalibrate, and realign.

We all have seasons of our souls. They are individual experiences we go through, and as we learn the stages, we free ourselves from angst, drama, and frustration. We soon learn we are never off track or behind. After I discovered what season my soul was in, I shifted my entire experience by accepting what was happening and aligning with the present moment. I started to repeat the mantra "Let me be still and listen to the truth" (which is Lesson 106 in *A Course in Miracles*). By turning to meditation and quieting my mind, I was able to set aside my ego's fear-based voice and listen instead to the voice of reason and truth.

When change comes roaring in, we grasp at what used to be our comfortable normalcy in the hope of feeling safe. But if we can recognize that change is actually the constant and growth is our fate, we can relax a little bit more into all of life. Transitions can be terrifying, especially if we don't see their value in our bigger picture. When things aren't going the way we hoped or the way they used to, it is because the Universe is asking us to take an alternate route. Often this new way of being can reveal itself in a transition; it is an invitation to reevaluate an area of your life that has become stale and no longer serves you.

Earlier in the book, I mentioned the saying "Every next level of your life will demand a refreshed version of you." Well, in my time of transition, the demands of the new me were commanding my attention. I had become the next-level me, and the Universe was gracefully trying to remove what no longer fit. But like a child not getting her way at the toy store, I kicked and screamed. I tried desperately to hold on to things that weren't even working, simply because it was what I knew. How often do we all do this? We hold on to what we know out of routine, even if it doesn't really feel good anymore. There is safety and comfort in the familiar, but there is no real growth. In general, we aren't comfortable with change unless we feel we can control it. Most of our anxiety and frustrations stem from our inability to adapt to change as our fear of the unknown sets in. We want to know how things will work out because we think certainty will provide peace—but this lesson teaches us to realize that we can be peaceful even in the unknown and in the transitions in life.

LIFE TRUTH: INNER PEACE DOES NOT COME FROM OUR CIRCUMSTANCES BUT THROUGH OUR CONNECTION TO DIVINE LOVE, WHICH IS ETERNAL.

If you are on a spiritual and personal growth journey, you will get to a point where the work starts to work you. When we get to this point, the only thing left to do is surrender. But for so many, surrendering can feel like giving up. Many of us want to feel better, and in an attempt to do so, we reach for something outside of ourselves. We want a new experience to help pull us out of a stuck, static, unpleasant state. Maybe you got fired from your job, or a sudden relationship change occurred, or your financial situation is overwhelming, or maybe you are going through a health crisis. Or perhaps you're like I was—flying high on living the good life, then suddenly, *bam*, anxiety comes crashing in on your positive parade. Life just keeps throwing us unexpected curve balls. Life is full of contrast, which always comes with an opportunity to realign and readjust. It is in the uncertain times that we are gifted the time and space to refocus, regroup, and rebalance.

It can be hard to see clearly through life's transitions. We often want to move out of this stuck, frustrating state, but we have no idea which direction to go. If you're in a frantic and uneasy position, the first thing you can do is surrender to the world as it is and let go of how you think your life is or was supposed to look.

When we move from one season of our soul into the next, anxiety can take hold and wrap us up in a vicious cycle of self-blame, worry, and panic, but catching yourself before this happens is key. We can stop the worry and inner panic by releasing the need to have it all figured out, and instead surrendering to the journey, knowing we are in a season that has a Divine Reason. This means wherever you are, you allow yourself to be there. We remove the judger who judges us for judging ourselves and relax more into the full experience of life. It's an opportunity to meet yourself where you are, not where your inner critic demands you should be. Because where you are, right now, is always enough.

The idea of your soul having seasons is inspired by Summer Bacon and the teaching of Dr. Peebles. In her book *Seasons of the Soul*, Bacon talks about the changes we go through as we grow. We can navigate the seasons of our soul by taking the opportunity to understand ourselves even more. In learning and understanding the seasons of your soul, you may discover a renewed faith in yourself, humanity, and the Universe. You won't grasp or hold on to things that are no longer working. You'll be happy to let go of what is no longer necessary because you will know and trust that what is coming next is even better than before. By understanding the key soul seasons, when the outside world seems chaotic and uncertain, you will obtain an inner balance, which will help you stay calm and centered.

The seasons of your soul are a lot like mini adventures, which are inspired and aligned with the rhythm of nature. As many wise sages, indigenous peoples, shamans, and gurus have known for centuries, nature is our best teacher. And just like with the seasons in nature, there are appropriate actions to take within each season of your soul. Each season invites in massive learning, compassion, and awareness. The four stages in both nature and the soul are clarification/decay (fall), completion/death (winter), development/exploration/fertilization (spring), and actualization/rebirth (summer). Using the stages of nature as a mirror, we can see the stages of our own personal growth and spiritual advancement.

THE FOUR MAIN STAGES & SEASONS OF YOUR SOUL

Releasing - Trusting - Surrender
Ask: What is no longer in alignment and needs to change?

Rest - Patience - Clarity - Releasing
Ask: What areas of my life need adjustments or fine-tuning?

Completion
(Death)
Winter

Development
Exploration
(Fertilization)
Spring

New Beginnings - Hope - Preparation
Ask: What does the true me need and want?

Clarification
(Decay)
Fall

Actualization
(Rebirth)
Summer

Reinvention - Alignment - Relief - Joy
Ask: How can I show up for myself in ways I never have before?

The Four Main Stages and Seasons of Your Soul

- Completion (Death) Winter
- Development/Exploration (Fertilization) Spring
- Actualization (Rebirth) Summer
- Clarification (Decay) Fall

SEASON 1: COMPLETION (DEATH) WINTER

Overview: Descend into the dark, surrender to stillness, honor the silence. It may seem odd to have completion as the first stage, but everything—including life—is a circular process. There is no real order to the stages; they all fold into one another.

LIFE TRUTH: THE ENDING OF ONE THING IS ALWAYS THE BEGINNING OF SOMETHING NEW.

The completion season often occurs during or right after a major, life-altering event, such as a breakup, divorce, being fired from a job, or receiving a disease diagnosis. Much like when a caterpillar is turning into a butterfly, it has no idea it will be reborn as a magnificent creature that flies; it simply cocoons itself into a cozy, warm place and surrenders to the death of the self it has known. The butterfly is the completion process of the caterpillar, representing a new layer of self, but there is always a space in between the old and new—the time in the cocoon, where it isolates and surrenders to the unknown. In relation to our own lives, this phase is a prime time to go inward and hibernate. What's really happening in this phase is a completion process. We have outgrown what we once knew and are being asked to go within ourselves so we can have enough strength and awareness to open up more authentically on the other side. Of all the phases, this is the most uncertain and dark, which can bring up our deepest fears. Unrest, regrouping, restructuring, and the falling away of the old all occur in this phase.

It helps to remind ourselves that we have arrived at a place in our lives where we have learned everything we needed on this level and have grown to our full capacity. This phase won't last forever, so focus on the light available within the darkness. New awareness and understanding are in our future, but we must surrender to the release and death of old pieces of us. This can include all aspects of our life that no longer work or serve us. This can be a trying time in life because this is a phase of conclusions, which means all things that must be resolved will be revealed. Essentially, this means that anything you haven't looked at or anything holding you back will come to the surface to be healed and transformed. But there's no need to worry, because really it is a completion of an aspect of yourself that is no longer needed—for where you are going, the old habits, thoughts, and beliefs cannot exist. Next-level you may not need the frustration in the mind over controlling your body weight, the pressure of a demanding job, the home in a location you don't feel connected to, the unfulfilling relationship, etc. Whatever it is you are being asked to let go of, honor the release. This can include habits, people, situations, attachments, addictions, and even perspectives.

Season of Completion Soul Alignment Session

This season is a time of deep inner alignment, rest, and renewal. You are releasing what no longer serves you. When in this phase, self-inquiry is the golden ticket forward.

Shadow side of the completion season:

- Feeling lost
- Sadness/depression
- Discomfort
- Anxiety/irritation
- Uncertainty

Bright side of the completion season:

- Release
- Allowing/acceptance
- Trust
- Possibilities
- Surrender

Questions to ask yourself in this phase are:

1. What am I clinging to or restricting?

2. What is no longer serving me or my highest good?

3. What is no longer in alignment and needs to change?

Opportunity:
Surrender to the moment and allow the unfolding. The purpose of this season is to expand by contracting. As you go inward and reflect, you will grow and heal, and this will help you expand into a more aligned version of you. Navigate the unsteady times with a quiet confidence and the inner knowing that all is in right order. Practice being present and listen to your body. The theme of this season is reset, renewal, and recharge. Meditation, self-reflection, and radical self-care will see you through.

SEASON 2: DEVELOPMENT/EXPLORATION (FERTILIZATION) SPRING

Overview: Awaken to your inner light and see the potential and growth opportunities all around you.
Soon enough, without much struggle, you will arrive at the exploration stage, which is a lot like spring. You've made it through the woods, you can see more clearly now, and you have hope again in your heart. Think of the farmer or gardener preparing the land for their plants; they must first pull out old weeds, till the soil, and then plant the seeds. This is a time of great inner strength that helps you access a new power within. In this season, you are setting the foundation for the future. You may have an abundance of clear ideas, visions, insights, and a new knowing that can help guide you forward. A realigning and energizing opportunity is underway. Results are yet to come to their fruition, but unlike during the last season, there is more light now, along with a deep trust and an internal knowing that the action steps you are taking

will lead to fulfillment. The new authentic parts of you that you were once afraid to show begin to feel more natural. You have more confidence in yourself and trust the new-level you. You are showing up as more fully actualized in the world. This is a time of honoring your true self and consistently showing up as authentically as you can. You start to see that it is safe to be you and that expressing yourself feels right. This season is all about exploring new ideas, concepts, and realities for you and your loved ones.

In this new phase, much like a baby learning how to walk, you are awakening and stumbling through a new world and new level of you. It is common for fear to step in and block you. Fear of growth and fear of failure rear up in this phase. You can easily overcome these doubts by returning to your heart and trusting this season of your soul. Take guided action, and remember that this stage is not about achieving your fullest potential but rather about planting the seeds for the life and vision you truly want to manifest. Like the gardener planting flowers, the seeds must go into the ground before they can grow. It is time to be intentional with your actions and only plant what you hope to experience. This is a time of grand thinking, practicing, learning, investing, and trusting both yourself and the Universe. It is about building a rock-solid foundation for long-term stability.

Season of Development/Exploration Soul Alignment Session

This season requires you to be present with yourself and the creative manifestation process. Be proactive in your self-exploration, and keep aligning and taking inspired action with what feels best for you.

Shadow side of the development/exploration phase:

- Overanalyzing, overthinking
- Feeling blocked
- Becoming paralyzed by choice
- Fear of failure or fear of growth

Bright side of the development/exploration phase:

- Birth, new beginnings
- Hope/excitement
- Adventure
- Preparation
- Self-expression

Questions to ask yourself in this phase are:

1. What is the future I am working to create?

2. What inspiration is coming to me?

3. What guiding action can I take today to help build the future I want?

4. What does the true me need and want?

Opportunity:
This is a super time to gather more ideas and start forming a clear vision and plan. Explore your abundant nature and let the creative power move through you into inspired action. Practice gratitude and joy as you appreciate what is going well.

SEASON 3: ACTUALIZATION (REBIRTH) SUMMER

Overview: Leap into your ideal life with joy and ease. Your new reality is supported by all that you have become.

It takes courage to show up and rebirth yourself, but as you will soon see, it is the most freeing part of your life journey. You have special skills, talents, and unique perspectives that can help you grow at a soul level and also help others. This is the phase where you see that by just being you, you get to make a positive impact on the world. This is a time of celebration and awareness. You may have a heightened intuition, and trusting yourself becomes much more natural. In this phase, you embody joy, for you are allowing your true essence to shine through. This is your space to manifest your dreams into existence. There is a universal, cosmic reassurance guiding you forward, helping you live with more ease. You have conquered your doubts and inner fears and healed yourself into an authentic you who is actualized in the world. You are now living as next-level you. Be proud of yourself and embrace this abundant pleasure.

Instead of asking, overanalyzing, and internalizing, in this season allow yourself to be more present in the revealing, honoring, and shining of your true self. You have done great work to arrive at this season, and you have great work to do. Your wings have expanded, and flying high requires a new level of understanding. This is when you finally embrace all you've been building up to. It might be a new career or business venture, a new relationship, or a lifelong dream actualized. Trust your own focus and take action with care. This is what you've been waiting for. You have a new perspective on patterns, situations, and experiences, and you begin to relate to the world in a more honest way, because you have transformed at your core. You now see that everything is connected and that there were always reasons for what you went through. You were never off track or behind, and everything needed to happen the way it did because it was always bringing you to this magnificent season of full self-actualization.

Season of Actualization Soul Alignment Session

This season requires you to spread your wings and be the fullest expression of your true self. Enjoy the excitement as your confidence is high and you are living your dream.

Shadow side of the actualization season:

- Overwork
- High expectations
- Misaligned energy
- Pressure

Bright side of the actualization season:

- Reinvention
- Flow
- Alignment
- Connection
- Joy, pleasure, and play
- Sense of relief and accomplishment

Questions to ask in this season are:

1. What am I grateful for, and what can I celebrate?

2. In what new ways do I want to express myself?

3. How can I show up for myself in ways I never have before?

4. How can I be more intentional with my choices and live with more purpose?

Opportunity:
This season is your fullest expression of self. Everything you have done has led you to this realization of all you are meant to be in this moment. You can now appreciate the fruits of your own labor.

SEASON 4: CLARIFICATION (DECAY) FALL

Overview: Fall into your inner angst, honor the shift.
Nothing lasts forever, even the good feelings of your actualized self. As you start to live with more purpose and alignment, you will step into the next phase of realignment, which is clarification. You have grown so much, which means the new you must be sustained for the long term, and the only way to do this is to reconnect inward to reevaluate and realign yourself with integrity and focus. Because you have grown, it is important to once again reassess what is and is not working in your life.

But because this season follows the blissed-out high of the actualization phase, you may resist the uncertainty that starts to boil within. The lack of confidence and a sense of decay is upon you; you may feel inklings of "something feels off," though you will question them because you are living everything you've worked for. Underlying anxieties surface in this unknown space, as it can bring up your unhealed fears of "I'm not good enough," "this is too good to be true," "I don't deserve this," etc.

The biggest struggle in this season is resistance. As the fog of the new season sets in, you want nothing more than to go back to breezy summer, but a brisk chill sets in and you enter the abyss of the unknown. You'll know when you've entered this season of your soul because you will feel a subtle inner pull of change. You will start to feel that certain things in your life feel off-kilter. The many things you worked towards no longer bring you the same satisfaction.

So many of us feel trapped and stuck when things just aren't flowing. Then what do we do? We fill our schedules with business, to-dos, meetings, and new projects. We don't stop and embrace the stillness; we refuse to allow ourselves to be present. This is the shadow side of this season. It's a time of unrest, confusion, and releasing. The purpose of this season is to prepare you for the hibernation of the next season, for your soul's optimal level of growth and expansion is upon you. Now is an excellent time to take stock and evaluate what still feels good and what's starting to feel stale in your life. You've reached the edge of your own growth potential from all you have previously been, and it is time to allow the restructuring to take place. Remember that *what is to come* is far greater than *what was*, even if *what was* was pretty great. Let go and trust so you can keep surrendering and trusting the process.

Season of Clarification Soul Alignment Session:

You've hit an experience plateau, and you may experience a growing sense of boredom and lack of motivation. You've outgrown what you once needed to grow into. Allow this season to align you with your optimal self. You are always growing and changing, so embrace the changing of the season and let yourself fall into the autumn season of your soul.

Shadow side of the clarification season:

- Boredom
- Confusion
- Unrest
- Lack of motivation

Bright side of the clarification season:

- More space
- Rest and revelation
- Patience and clarity
- Releasing

Questions to ask yourself in this phase are:

1. What kind of life do I really want to live?

2. Who have I become? Who do I want to be?

3. What areas of my life need adjustments or fine-tuning?

4. Where have I been hiding from myself or afraid to show up more fully?

Opportunity:
Try your best to trust the process. This is actually a magnificent time of you realigning even more deeply with your true self. Your hidden fears of the unknown may surface, but trust their unfolding. Know that the Universe is supporting and guiding you. Practice self-love and self-care and trust your intuition and self. Believe in the power of all that you are by following the inner guidance from your heart. Knowing the seasons of your soul can provide a fabulous road map to understanding your current situation. Whatever you are going through, there is a reason—because you are in this specific season.

It is important to note that the seasons of your soul don't necessarily correlate with the exact seasons of nature in real time, and they don't always last for the same amount of time as a season in nature does. Also, as you move from one season to the next, you may experience a variety of symptoms. Between each season of your soul is an ascension process, during which you may experience what I call *inner growth symptoms* or *ascension symptoms*. This is an energetic experience where the universal vibrational energy forces you to rise above the old habits and narrow views you had at your old level of existence. You are healing and growing and learning more about yourself, and this brings about new realities. With this comes physical, emotional, and mental changes. I discuss common symptoms you may experience during the ascension process in the first action step at the end of this lesson.

As you go through life, the seasons of your soul cycle into one another, and you constantly evolve into a higher vibrational version of you. The more you learn, the more you actually unlearn what you've been taught or what has been passed onto you. As you step more fully into your awakening—the real you—the truth will be revealed to you. Any cultural conditioning, indoctrination, or limiting beliefs will reveal themselves so you can move past these illusions and heal. By participating actively in your own personal growth journey and saying you are ready for more, you will grow into a more authentic place.

Let's put this lesson into practice:

These steps are designed to help you navigate the seasons of your soul. To implement this lesson, Your Soul Has Seasons, try these steps.

Step 1: Accept the invitation to grow.
We are always growing into more of who we really are, but you must actively participate in this growth process. The seasons of your soul can serve as a delicate road map to guide you forward. There is no such thing as "off track" or "behind," as you are always in an upward growth cycle. Instead of focusing on feelings of lack or what is not working, think about how far you have come and what you are growing into.

As you grow into the next season of your soul, you may experience inner growth, or ascension, symptoms. Here is a list of some of the ascension and inner growth symptoms that impact us between and during our seasons of our soul:

- Feeling exhausted, overwhelmed, or anxious
- Experiencing intense energy and high levels of stress or euphoria
- A feeling of disorientation
- Unusual aches and pains throughout different parts of your body
- Odd sleep patterns and vivid dreams
- "Seeing" and "hearing" things
- Loss of identity
- No longer trusting or believing in old patterns and beliefs
- Feeling "out of body"
- Heightened sensitivities to your surroundings
- Lack of motivation
- Sudden changes in habits and routines
- Experiencing emotional ups and downs
- Feeling more peace, joy, and ease
- Stressing less and having more energy
- Experiencing more clarity of thought and focused intent
- Feeling an inner drive to help, assist, and support others
- Experiencing a sense of ease where there was once struggle
- Feeling more balanced, calm, and grounded

Recognize that each new season of your soul will invite new growth symptoms. Be patient with yourself, and know that it is all part of the process to align back to your true nature.

Step 2: Release resistance. Allow.
Allow the unfolding in your life. You will get to a place where you realize resistance will no longer work. Stop fighting the flow, and instead relax into it and allow the natural seasons of your soul to exist. It is all part of the beautiful journey called your life. Embrace each phase.

Step 3: Be present. Be still.

One of the most important ways to navigate the seasons of your soul and any ascension symptoms is to be present. There is no need to judge what comes up, but rather allow and surrender to the current moment. You will find an unbelievable peace in the present moment as you accept that all is in right order and there is never anything to fear—because everything we go through is part of a process to guide us to more love, truth, and joy.

Step 4: Trust Divine Alignment and Flow.

Above all else, what helped me the most through my difficult transitions was tapping into the rhythm of the Universe and trusting Divine Flow. You can develop the ability to let go and dive deeper into life, allowing each experience to be what it is, instead of what you think it needs to be. With that said, many of us believe that growing requires suffering. But as the Buddhist tradition explains, our only suffering is one of attachment. In this sweet surrender, you allow the personal growth to take hold. In Sanaya Roman's book *Spiritual Growth: Being Your Higher Self,* she explains, "The easier you can let go of the old, and embrace the new, the more you can learn through joy rather than struggle. Approach change as a great adventure. Believe that all change is for your highest good or it wouldn't be happening."[21] You can always ask the Universe for help when things seem overwhelming. Prayer, meditation, and journaling are solid tools to guide you forward.

Questions to ask:

1. What is no longer working, and what can I release and let go of?

2. What season of the soul am I in?

3. What aspects of my life need fine-tuning?

---

21 Samaya Roman, *Spiritual Growth: Being Your Higher Self* (Tiburon, CA: HJ Kramer, 1992).

As you start to live with more intention by understanding the seasons of your own soul, you will discover a deeper sense of self-worth, love, and compassion. In the next lesson, you will learn about your ultimate life purpose and your true reason for being. This is one of my favorite lessons; it contains the process I used personally to heal from depression, drug addiction, eating disorders, and extreme anxiety, and it is the same process I use in my coaching practice and retreats to help clients align with their true self and live their life purpose with more passion. I look forward to sharing it with you.

LESSON 7

YOUR PURPOSE IS
PERSONAL EXPANSION

In 2009, I was diagnosed with clinical depression, but something I've never shared openly is that I was also diagnosed with borderline bipolar disorder. At the time, I was stuck in a toxic relationship, silently suffering from eating disorders and drug addiction, and trapped in a career that was suffocating my soul. I didn't know it at the time, but that diagnosis was one of the most important things that happened to me, as it forever changed the trajectory of my life. I came home that night and cried on the bathroom floor. Lying on the cold tile, soaked in my own tears, I pleaded for help. I said, "I can't do this anymore. It is exhausting to live this life that doesn't feel good." And in that moment, the air thinned out, and I felt a calm, loving presence wrap around me. For the first time in decades, I felt safe. I heard the words *Follow your heart*. And every day since that moment, I have committed to following my heart, which has led to the most miraculous life of joy, abundance, fulfillment, love, support, and freedom.

Something else that I haven't shared is why that day was so impactful for me. It was the presence that visited me that day that forever changed my life. I felt connected to something bigger than me—more peace and love—and in experiencing that connection, I knew I needed more of it. Angels, God, my higher self, the Universe, my ancestors, ascended masters—whatever it was, I knew that that was my path forward through the uncertainty and fear.

In trusting this presence, I took daily action to transform my life. The more I connected to my spiritual side, the more balanced I felt. Over the next decade, I went on my own spiritual journey and learned how to trust my intuition and believe in myself and the Universe, and my life has become an amazing experience. It was the feeling of the loving presence that really stayed with me, but equally important was the message I received: *Follow your heart.*

LIFE TRUTH: WHEN YOU FOLLOW YOUR HEART, YOU ARE ALWAYS PROVIDED FOR.

I knew that listening to and trusting my heart was a key component to getting unstuck and living a fulfilled life. One of the most important things we can do to feel better and live a life of more meaning, connection, and peace is to step into our purpose. Every single one of us has a purpose, yet so many of us are afraid to live it. Whether it is fear that it won't work out and we'll fail, or worry about the amount of time, money, and energy it may take, we stay stuck in our routines. But I learned firsthand that ignoring our true calling can harm us in myriad ways. For me, it manifested in drug addiction, eating disorders, and anxiety attacks. When the doctor diagnosed me with depression and borderline bipolar disorder, my first thought was *Finally. Now I know what is wrong with me. There is a name for it.* I thought since the world had a name for it, and there was a pill I could take, then it meant it could be fixed.

But when I went home that night, something didn't feel right. I had the prescription in hand, but I didn't really identify with the diagnoses the doctor had given me. I started doing my own research, and over the next several years, I visited naturopaths, Reiki masters, spiritual gurus, and shamans. I personally worked with some of the world's top healers, flying all around the globe to seek out universal Life Truths, and through all of this journeying, I realized that nothing was actually wrong with me except the denial of my own true nature. It became clear to me that my depression was an oppression of self. (Just to note: as we discovered in a previous lesson, everyone is on their own journey, and I know for some, a diagnosis such as depression and bipolar disorder can also be due to a chemical imbalance or a myriad of other factors. But in my case, I discovered that it was due to a disconnect from my true nature and Source Energy.) I was out of alignment by not honoring my deepest needs. I didn't know it at the time, but I am an empath.

An empath is someone who is highly aware of the emotions of those around them, to the point of feeling those emotions themselves. When I was diagnosed with depression and bipolar disorder, I didn't realize that I was picking up on all the toxic energy in my workplace and the city I lived in. I would go out with friends, only to come home and cry myself to sleep. I thought it was my own emotions, but as a highly sensitive person, I empathically felt into others and took on their pain as my own. In learning how to work with this trait, I have learned that our environment can shape our experiences. And as empaths, if we aren't aware of our own empathic nature, we may feel like something is wrong with us or even become depressed or suicidal. I have since learned that being an empath is one of the most beautiful gifts a human can have. We can compassionately care for others and nurture those who can't always process their own pain. The difference now for me is knowing my empathic nature and seeing it as a skill set that I can master instead of a debilitation or limitation. Dr. Judith Orloff, a pioneer in the emotional field, describes empaths as those who absorb the world's joys and stresses like "emotional sponges."

Over the years, I've had many people reach out to me asking, "What are you doing to speak out against social injustices? What is your stance on this issue or current event? What are you doing to help combat global warming? What is your political affiliation?" The list goes on with people wanting to know how I will use my voice and my platform to stand up against certain issues and help move us forward. Of course, these issues are all important to me, but how I chose to show up was often different from the preferred methods of the people who were asking me. When I first begain receiving these messages, I would respond to them, but it quickly became clear to me that nothing I said was ever enough for people who were focused on asking others what they were doing instead of honoring their own path.

Chapter 29 in *A Course in Miracles* says, "Seek not outside yourself. For it will fail." Every time we look to others to see what they are doing, it takes us off our own path and out of alignment. All of us have an important part to play in the rich tapestry of life and the evolution of humanity. And if we all do our own part and trust that others are doing their part the best they know how (instead of needing others to do what we think is best), we can move forward collectively. When each of us honors our own skills, talents, and innate gifts, we can position ourselves to be of the highest service to others. All of us are born with a unique set of gifts, talents, and skills that are woven into the fabric of our collective lives. When we live from authenticity, we come into harmony with all of life as we express the Divine Love we are.

LIFE TRUTH: WHEN WE LIVE OUR PURPOSE, WE ARE ALIGNING WITH THE FIELD OF ENERGY THAT SUPPORTS ALL OF LIFE.

I struggled for many years trying to find my "purpose" until I realized we don't have to find anything; we simply allow and reveal. And the purpose for all of us is expansion. We expand into our calling by feeling into what is best for us. In the movie *Thrive II: This Is What It Takes*, Foster Gamble discusses the importance of each one of us living our purpose by understanding where we fit. Foster Gamble and his team have identified thirteen Sectors that cover all areas of human activity, which are all interconnected.[22] By identifying key problems in each of these Sectors and coming up with solutions, we can create a thriving world, together in harmony.

Here are the thirteen Sectors:

---

22   Thriveon.com, "THRIVE Solutions Model: A Guide for Self-Organizing in Communities," accessed July 27, 2021, thriveon.com/THRIVE-Solutions-Model.pdf.

The Sector Wheel

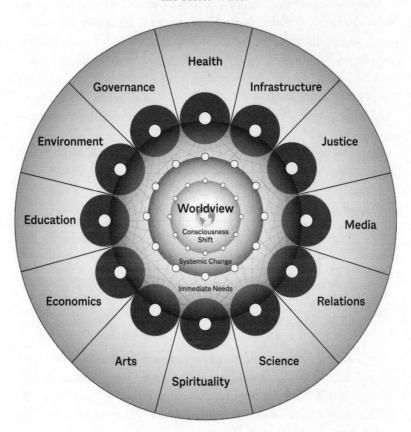

thriveon.com

1. Health	8. Arts
2. Infrastructure	9. Economics
3. Justice	10. Education
4. Media	11. Environment
5. Relations	12. Governance
6. Science	13. Worldview
7. Spirituality	

After looking at the Sectors wheel, ask yourself what areas you are most drawn to. For me, spirituality, arts, and education are where I teach and lead from. (For you, it may be justice, health, environment, etc.) In this way, we all fit together in the cosmic earth web like a puzzle, and if we each focus on our own alignment within each Sector, we will live a life of more purpose and joy, and we can all thrive. When we are all doing our part, we will be in harmony and one with the natural laws of the Universe.

After you identify what you are most drawn to (and it can be a few Sectors), you can then look at the issues in that area and identify what best matches your skills and areas of passion. Then, look to where you feel called to take action. Here are the main areas to take action in:

1. Immediate Needs

2. Systemic Change

3. Consciousness Shift

For instance, do you want to support immediate needs and be on the ground helping to feed the hungry or caring for those affected directly by tragedies? When I was diagnosed with depression, the first thing I did was focus on what I loved. I love animals, so I volunteered at a local animal shelter, which led to the adoption of my new (at the time) best friend, Tucker, who helped further pull me out of depression and into my happiness. By focusing on the immediate needs of animals who needed help, I was connecting to my own purpose. Perhaps you feel drawn toward creating systemic changes within your chosen Sectors. Do you feel called to protest, create petitions, go to town meetings, or look into changing laws related to your Sectors? Or maybe you want to work on creating a shift in consciousness; teachers, writers, philosophers, and artists often serve from this area. The final focus is on affecting worldview. Maybe you feel drawn to help others see the realities of the world or to help them shift into a new awareness of what is possible through changing their worldview. All these aspects are needed, and there is no wrong way to help as long as we are aligned with our own personal path. We all fit together like puzzle pieces, and doing what you love can help to uplift and serve the entire planet. But it's important to recognize that each person has a role to play, and needing others to play in your box is not the goal. Your life purpose is to expand and grow, and we can do this by identifying our passion and living it with more intention and purpose.

To help us understand this concept in even more depth, we can lean on the Japanese concept of ikigai. The term *ikigai* is composed of two Japanese words: *iki*, referring to "life," and *kai*, which roughly means "the realization of what one expects and hopes for." Essentially, ikigai is "reason for being." So, my dear, what is your reason for being?

How to find your ikigai:

Even if you are already clear about your life purpose, asking these questions can often help you realign with the truth. Take a moment to draw your own version of the overlapping circles of the *ikigai* symbol and consider the following:

- What do you love? (your passion)
- What aspects of your life bring you into your heart? When do you feel most alive?
- What are you great at? (your mission)
- What unique skills do you have that come most naturally to you? What talents have you cultivated? What do you excel at even when you aren't trying?
- What does the world need? What cause do you believe in? (your vocation)
- What breaks your heart or pulls at your gut? What change would you most love to create in the world? What would you give your life for?
- What do/can people value and pay you for? (your profession)
- What service, value, or offering do you bring, or could you bring, that provides real value to others? Something people need and are happy to pay for or share something of value in exchange?

When we align all of these areas, we are living our purpose, on purpose. We are expanding ourselves into the mission we are put on Earth for. I believe most of the disharmony within ourselves—depression, disease, addictions, and imbalances—is often caused because we are denying ourselves our true nature. We are not honoring our true path. Your true path is your purpose and reason for being. When you align with it, your life will flow. Now, this doesn't mean everything happens overnight or that you won't have hardships along the way. Living a life of purpose—on purpose—is about authenticity and expanding your own potential, but it doesn't free you from earthbound realities such as paying the bills and working through karma. But when you align with your heart, things do become easier, and with time, you will be making a living doing what you love. Think about how you feel when you do what you love; you are present and fully in the moment, time expands, and you are free from the pressures of this world. Doing what you love becomes an act of service to the world. It takes time, but when you live from your heart, you will always be supported, and you will feel more connected to all of life, which in turn helps provide for you in myriad ways. Synchronicities begin to flow, and the Universe guides your every move.

Another way you can activate your authentic purpose is by understanding the concept of *sacred activism*. This encourages us to find our purpose by "following our heartbreak." Andrew Harvey, who coined the term, calls us to discover that which is most deeply disturbing in our world and to use this as a catalyst to propel our actions and discover where we can make the biggest difference. For example, I suffered through a disassociation with self that caused depression, anxiety, drug addictions, and eating disorders. In experiencing these situations firsthand, I found an internal fuel to help those who still suffer in these areas. My heartache and heartbreak turned into the activation of a deeper calling within to use this experience and help others. Many of us go through extremely difficult life situations and traumas so we can understand them, and as we make our way through the healing process and overcome them, we often feel called to use our own experience to help others.

In my business mentor program, the most successful and fulfilled clients are the ones who use their personal experience to help others. When Annie first came to me, she was positioning herself as a corporate business coach, but it wasn't flowing for her. She had a difficult time getting and retaining clients, and she felt stuck. Together, we looked at her personal experience and what she had been through. She shared her personal story of surviving her son's suicide and suffering through the diagnosis of a disease that runs in her family—on top of going through a divorce. I shared the sacred activism concept with her, explaining how these pivotal moments of her life have strengthened her so she can now help others. She experienced an instant aha moment and said, "I can help those who are going through trauma and survivors of suicide or the death of loved ones. I know firsthand what they are experiencing; therefore, I can better help support them." When we talked on the phone the following week, she had restructured her coaching business and already had two new paying clients, and she had started an online community for suicide support survivors. She took her passion to the stage and later became a TEDx speaker, sharing her own experience of how trauma turned into mission work.

Your personal experience is the greatest credibility you have. Many people go to school and take classes on subjects to advance their awareness, but personal experience will always trump these certificates of approval. In fact, today's top masters, gurus, thought leaders, and shamans almost all went through some type of extreme hardship and suffering. For example, Tony Robbins was homeless and lived in his car before becoming a world-renowned personal growth guru. With respect, it is all connected—your past, present, and future are all tied to advancing yourself so you can be of service to others.

LIFE TRUTH: YOUR PERSONAL EXPERIENCE IS THE CATALYST FOR BEING OF THE HIGHEST SERVICE TO OTHERS.

When you are living your purpose and doing what you love, you are helping others. Have you ever looked at nature to really see the rhythm of it all? Everything is at the service of the greater web of life. Observe how the plants, air, water, and all of the elements work together to help support, nurture, and uplift one another. The tree is rooted deep into the soil, from which it gets its nutrients and which is home to the earthworms and other bugs. The rain waters the tree, and the tree gives food and shelter to animals and bugs, and those animals become part of the greater ecosystem. All is connected, and all is of service to everything else. It is a divine dance of life.

The same is true for human beings; we are part of that symbiotic, harmonious experience. We have an opportunity to hone our own gifts and perspectives to help support and serve all of life. Those who are the happiest and the most at peace are usually helping others—not because it's something that looks good on a résumé but because it genuinely gives them life force. To serve is to love, and we all want more love in our life.

LIFE TRUTH: EVERYTHING THAT EXISTS IS FOR THE PURPOSE OF SUPPORTING ALL OF LIFE.

When you step into this power, you see how everything is connected and one with everything else. The purpose of this viewpoint is to see that you are love and then apply that to your life with everything you do. This way of living creates an expansion of balance, harmony, beauty, and peace. Ask yourself what you personally feel called to do. How can you serve today? What disturbing things in the world affect you the most? Especially if you are an empath, feel into which areas impact you the most. These can be powerful indicators of what you are put on Earth to do.

If you still struggle with what your purpose is, focus on what you have been through. One of the first things I do with life-coaching clients who want to live with more purpose is ask them what their pivotal moments are. Pivotal moments are key periods in your life when a fundamental shift or radical change happened. What experience did you go through that helped you become who you are today? My pivotal moment was being diagnosed with depression, which led to the fulfilling life I lead today. Another pivotal moment was dealing with my anxiety and panic attacks after doing this work for years, which cracked me open for an even deeper awareness of self and my connection to all of life, which led to my writing this book.

List your pivotal moments and ask yourself, "Who was I before that situation happened? Then, who was I after?" This insight can help guide you forward. Philosopher and civil rights leader Howard W. Thurman said, "Don't ask what the world needs. Ask what makes you come alive and do that . . . Because what the world really needs is people who have come alive." The bottom line is that when you do what you love, you are living your purpose, and this is the ultimate form of personal growth and expansion.

LIFE TRUTH: YOU DON'T HAVE TO FIND YOUR PURPOSE. JUST ALLOW IT TO EXPAND WITHIN YOU.

Alongside our passions that lead to our life purpose, we also all have a soul purpose. We are here on planet Earth to grow and evolve our own consciousness, and our souls are always growing. Your human self has a purpose, but your soul has a mission as well. We come to Earth for a variety of reasons to help our ascension process.

Life Purposes Your Soul May Experience

To Finish and Clear Karmic Relationships

In Hinduism and Buddhist philosophies, karma is the foundation of everything. It is our destiny resulting in our actions. Basically, what you do unto others, you do to yourself—if not in this life, then in the next. With this understanding, there are people in your life you have agreed to meet in this lifetime. Some become lifelong relationships; others are quick assignments. All relationships are assignments, and when we meet up with people who push our buttons, frustrate us, or cause us emotional distress, it is often karma balancing out. We are clearing past life situations. The same is true for relationships that aren't stressful or dramatic. You may have a friend or family member who feels peaceful and safe to be around. When you are with one another, life feels good, safe, and gentle, and you can be your truest self. This is a gift you are both giving to one another, and it is often a karmic relationship in which you agreed to be each other's break from the harsh realities of the world. All relationships are important to our life. No matter how long they last, they are part of your soul's growth. And most of us will have karmic situations to heal.

To Discover the Beauty in All

Another reason we come to Earth is to explore beauty in the physical world. It's possible to see the beauty in everything, although this is a rather difficult lesson to learn. When we are in our heads—the analytical, observant, categorizing aspect of us—it can be easy to pass judgment on things that seem wrong. There is hate, corruption, manipulation, terrorism, greed, and unethical people. We can see this as darkness, but the darkness will always be overcome by light. If you are here to discover the beauty of it all, it's possible you've experienced tremendous hardship, pain, trauma, abuse, and suffering in this life or in past lives. Through this hardship, you have an opportunity to seek out love and beauty. You can learn more compassion and love for yourself and others. When we are abused, we often don't hate the abuser; we hate ourselves. This can lead to a lifetime of learning how to love yourself through the contrast. For example, spiritual teacher Teal Swan suffered a tremendously abusive childhood at the hands of a ritualistic cult that targeted her because of her God-given gifts. She was physically and emotionally abused for years, but she overcame this part of her life and now uses her gifts for the greater good by sharing tools and spiritual teachings on YouTube and in books, workshops, and retreats. She works every day to see the beauty in it all, but her life purpose came from healing from a difficult past. We may look at things and think there is a clear line, or that it's easy to declare right and wrong, ugly versus pretty, but as a spiritual being having a human experience, our true essence knows that everything can be beautiful if we see it with love.

To Explore Abundance and Learn What Is Important

Abundance isn't always financial gain and power; it can be an attitude in which you live your life. Feeling abundant is your true nature, for you know you are always taken care of and provided for. Living your life through the eyes of Source love will give you access to the internal power of overwhelming love, and this is the true abundance we all seek—to know we are accepted and loved unconditionally as we are. From that place of knowing, we attract all we need and want. Life becomes richer because we are living from a place of worth and abundance instead of lack. Still, many follow a lifestyle in which they focus on money, success, fame, and popularity. We believe that getting these outward markers of shallow abundance will give us what we truly need, but we all eventually learn that money, stuff, and being in the public eye are not who we really are and not what truly matters. Still, it is a lesson many sign up to learn and choose to explore through the contrast. If you focus on money a lot and feel a lack when it comes to finances, or if you have a lot of money but still feel empty, you could be here to learn about the true source of abundance.

To Transcend the Ego

We all have egos—it is the part of us that judges, criticizes, and lives in fear. The ego is not a bad thing, as it helps us grow, but detaching from the ego and recognizing its limitations is an important part of the soul journey. Many of us become more aware of our ego when we step onto our spiritual path. Ego isn't always self-importance, but it is often the scared inner part of us. It's the part of us that experiences and reacts to the outside world and often tries to protect us, but it does this by keeping us small. We dim our light and shy away from showing our true self when we listen to our ego. Learning how to transcend this fear-based part of us can help us reach peace. Experiencing low self-esteem and lacking self-confidence are signs the ego is running the show. Learning how to love yourself and practicing self-compassion is a great way to transcend the ego, which is something many of us are here to learn.

Loving yourself is not egotistical—though for years we were taught it was—but it is the Divine path to fulfillment. Self-love is compassion and kindness to self, not a righteous focus on celebrating yourself over others. There are two spiritual paths we have a choice to take: service to ourselves or service to others. When our ego is in control, we are self-serving, and the love for self is because we think we are God. This is a manipulative ego trick of control. Once your ego recognizes God's love is within you, it diminishes, and your service to others becomes a path of empowerment and joy.

To Experience an Awakening

Perhaps you came to Earth to live a life where you open up to your spiritual self and experience an awakening. People who have near-death experiences often report being asleep, unconscious, or unaware of their spiritual nature until after their brush with death. Then, with a glimpse of their true power, they are awakened and see their life as a gift, and that it's an honor and a truly magnificent experience to be alive. Many of us go through a spiritual awakening where we realize that who we were is no longer who we truly are. The job titles, the relationship status, the superficial things we defined ourselves by don't truly matter when it comes to our true value within. Our love and light are the ultimate truth, and awakening to this new reality could be our main lesson in this life. Furthermore, when we define ourselves by outside situations—how many likes and followers we have on social media, the amount of money in our bank account, etc.—we lose sight of our truth. We are not anything outside of ourselves—all of that is fleeting. This is why when we lose those external things, we often lose sight of ourselves. When this happens, we have an opportunity to go inward and really discover who we are, and this leads to a spiritual awakening.

To Heal and Grow the Collective Consciousness

If you feel a strong desire to help others and your time on Earth feels mission driven, you could be here to help raise the collective consciousness. We do this through our teaching, art, writing, creativity, music, performance, and personal experiences. When you heal yourself, you get to a place where you feel you have to help others do the same. You want to help reduce their pain and show them what is possible. Not everyone has this desire, but if you want to help others and are a coach, teacher, healer, light worker, creative, or leader, it is pretty certain you are here to help humanity evolve.

But helping others and living your purpose doesn't have to be a grand gesture. You don't have to lead retreats or open up your own healing center (though if you feel guided to do so, trust this and by all means go for it), but you could simply add more love to your day-to-day actions. Walking the dog and smiling at the neighbors, allowing someone to go in line ahead of you at the store, being kind in your mind to the person who just cut you off while driving or who is driving very slow in front of you, talking in the elevator to strangers. Practicing kindness, compassion, patience, self-love, and awareness are just as powerful if not more so than aiming to heal humanity as a whole. The thing about light workers is, we sometimes become frustrated because we feel that there is so much more to do, that we aren't helping enough people. We want to help and heal others, but this is an enormous amount of pressure that we put on ourselves, which is unnecessary. You are not required to do anything but to practice more love in your life, and being kind to yourself when you look in the mirror is a great start. This in itself will raise the vibration and love on the planet more than anything else. Everything has to start with you. When you love yourself, you are adding more love into the world, and this helps heal and raise the collective consciousness.

To Know and Be Your True Self

You may have experienced lifetimes, even this one, in which you sacrificed yourself to care for or be there for others. Maybe you were afraid to show up and shine your true light. Or maybe you did share your true self and something bad happened. But shying away from your real self is not in store for you in this lifetime. You are here to know who you really are and experience yourself in ways you never have. Perhaps you love personal development; maybe you enjoy journaling and are always seeking more self-awareness. Learning to be yourself is a spiritual journey that takes courage and often lifetimes to master. It is one of the most precious life lessons because so many of us are terrified of knowing who we really are and are worried about what others will think. The path of the true-self warrior is to work through this fear and to discover the freedom in knowing and being your true self.

If you are working on yourself and growing personally, you are on a path of knowing who you really are. Your true self is amazing and ready to be more visible in the world. Don't wait until it's too late to learn this lesson. You are magnificent, and it's time the world sees this. Ultimately, though, it doesn't matter what others think of you, because when you are living from your true nature, you will be connected to the love in your heart and living in the Divine's image. And that is the most important love of all. Knowing and being your true self is not selfish but self-fulfilling, as to know yourself is to know your true essence of love and light, which brings you that unshakable inner peace. I love how Wayne Dyer explains it in his book *There's a Spiritual Solution to Every Problem*: "When you are an instrument of peace, you are not seeking anything, you are a peace provider. You do not seek peace by looking into the lives of others and wishing that they would change so you could become more peaceful. Rather you bring your own sense of calm to everyone you encounter."[23]

To Play and to Explore Contrast

Have you ever met someone who doesn't seem to get too serious about anything? They may be more interested in play and lighthearted things. Maybe they laugh a lot and know how to brighten the mood and lighten up your day. They don't get too involved with drama, and they avoid diving too deeply into anything. They are exploring life and just enjoying trying things. Maybe you relate; if you've had a lot of jobs or bounce around from place to place, you could be here to have fun and explore the layered opportunities of Earth. Some may call people like you drifters, hippies, or nomads, but you know you are here to maximize your time on Earth and stick your head into all things that feel fun. If you relate, you most likely don't want to take anything too seriously because you know life is short. You want to try as many things as you can before you leave Earth. This could involve myriad explorations, from hobbies and jobs to relationships and places you live. The more you experience, the more fulfilled you are. Have fun playing with the world. You are living your mission.

On the flip side, you may find yourself always involved with drama and stuck in difficult situations. You could be here to really understand and explore contrast. The planet Earth is a school of contrast, so no matter what your true purpose is, you will experience contrast through all of these avenues. But remember: the contrast we explore is designed to lead us to clarity.

---

23 Wayne W. Dyer, *There's a Spiritual Solution to Every Problem* (New York: HarperColllins, 2001), 146.

Let's put this lesson into practice:

These steps will help you activate this lesson, Your Purpose Is Personal Expansion.

Step 1: Break up with "The One."
Many of us struggle because we try to find that *one* thing that we are meant to do, but trying to find only one thing is the reason we feel like something is missing. The notion that we have only one thing we are meant for limits us from fulfilling our greatness. Start getting in touch with your passions! When you lead a passionate life, you are living your life on purpose. The one thing you can do to live with more passion and purpose is to experience life. Live the full journey. The purpose of life is to suck in the entire experience and love fully from the heart. This is why we are here: to learn to grow and become more of who we are. And we can only do this by exploring, growing, and experiencing life in a variety of ways. Thinking there is only one specific purpose actually keeps you from reaching your passion-fueled life.

Step 2: Turn your core passion into purpose.
Your heart is your best tool to access your true purpose and passion. Ask yourself what you love. Start taking steps to do what you love more often. When you are inspired and connected to your happy self, inspiration floods your heart and soul. When you lead from your heart, you are naturally more joyful and motivated to explore. By doing what you love, you will be inspired and gain insights into what brings you the most joy.

Make sure to separate your hobbies from your passion. You may love to paint or garden, but that doesn't mean you want to make a living doing it. Most folks get confused about finding their life purpose because they assume their hobbies are what brings them joy. Hobbies are joy moments that provide a sanctuary from our hectic life, but they aren't always our life purpose (in some cases they are, but not always), whereas passion has a hold on you. It keeps you up at night excited with ideas. You can't not do it. Passion is what you feel born to do. If you can separate the two, it's easier to move forward with more clarity. A good rule of thumb is to remember that passion fuels your soul. You're going to align with it naturally, so you might as well do it for a living.

Step 3: Get more clarity and confidence by taking more action. You can't think your way into finding your life purpose; you have to do/act your way into it. The more we take action, the clearer we get on things. So instead of overthinking it—"Will this work out? Should I try that? What if I don't like it? What if I don't make money at it?"—start taking steps toward your goals and start trying new things. I often say to my coaching clients that "We learn the way on the way" and "Action brings clarity." This means the more steps you take, the more clarity you get. This mindset will help you get out of your own way. I struggled for years trying to find out what my purpose was. This cycle only created a deeper lack of clarity. It wasn't until I started *doing* that things changed for me. I began writing and sent a story to *Chicken Soup for the Soul.* The second I received the letter of acceptance for my first-ever published story was unlike any moment before. Love flooded into my heart, and I knew that this was what I had to do with my life. I had to start writing to learn that my biggest passion was indeed writing. That only came with consistent action.

Clarity comes through the process of exploring, and action is where we get results. Most of us get amazing ideas, and we don't act on them because we immediately jump to how long it will take; or how much money, time, or energy it might require to produce that goal; or what others will think or say. But as author and motivational speaker Mastin Kipp says, "If there is an outcome you fear and you do not take action, you will produce the outcome you fear." Take action, and you will move through the fear blocking you. Ask yourself, "What inspiration can I act on?"

Step 4: Believe in your future self.
Finding your purpose and passion is a lot like a road trip. If you have ever taken a trip across the country, then you know you have a destination, but you can't always see the entire path or way to get there. You drive along the road, and sometimes construction or detours cause you to change course. You ultimately know you are on your way to the new destination, but the

real reward is how you get there. So many of us feel a desperate need to have it figured out; we need to know our purpose, and because we don't, we feel something is missing. But we often gloss over the path that leads us to finding our purpose—which is unfortunate, for it is this path that leads us to ourselves.

The turning point for every person who has crossed over into living a passionate life is the moment they start believing in something they can't see yet. We have to believe that our life can become better even if we don't see traces of it in our current reality. Instead of looking at what is not working, we can learn how to passionately push toward a better reality. This is the same for any situation in life that we want to improve. For example, if you are in an unhealthy relationship, you have to believe that you are deserving of and can be in a healthy, love-filled partnership.

You hold your attention on what you want, not what is. If you are in a job you dislike, but you don't know what job would make you happy, you can start by reaching for the hope that there is something better for you. Feeling hopeless is the fastest way to kill your passion and prevent you from finding your purpose. So how do you find hope in hopeless situations? You find inspiration to keep going by turning your attention to love instead of fear. You turn to trust in yourself and the Universe.

Questions to ask:

1. How can I be more intentional with my choices and live more on purpose?

2. Where am I being called to serve and support others?

3. Where is my heart guiding me, and what guided action can I take today?

4. How can I actively participate in creating a more harmonious world?

It is such an incredible experience to be who you are truly meant to be and live your Divine Purpose. Ultimately the purpose for us all is to expand and grow and realize our true nature is sourced from Divine Love. This is the reason we are here, and as you explore more of your true self, you will notice new dreams and goals emerging. In the next lesson, we will go through a process to help you address any physical, emotional, or spiritual barriers blocking you from receiving and giving the true gifts you are destined for.

LESSON 8

IN ORDER TO RECEIVE,
YOU MUST RELEASE

On my own personal healing journey, I've had the opportunity to work with wise healers, shamans, and mystics. One of the most profound healing ceremonies I've ever done was plant medicine in the form of ayahuasca. Plant medicine is said to shine a spotlight straight into the massive gap between who you think you are and who you truly are. My ayahuasca experience showed me all the ways I hide from the world and myself. It seems when we go searching for solutions and possibilities, we must first see our limitations. This is pretty common with any deep healing work we embark on, especially with sacred plant medicine and shaman work. In order to advance in our life, we have to look honestly at who we have become. To welcome new growth, we must see clearly all the areas that are not working and release their invisible power over us. Whether you fly to the jungle to work with shamans in an ayahuasca ceremony, work with a therapist or life coach, journal, or read a book on your own way to freedom, the healing journey is very personal for each individual, and it is never over or complete. What we seek on our healing journeys is truth and new awareness. The truth can be alarming, but only when we don't use the information to advance ourselves forward.

When you go on any deep healing journey, you will inevitably meet pieces of yourself that have been long abused, hidden, and tucked into the background. In plant medicine ceremonies, this is called the *purging*, and it is an integral part of the process. Purging can come in many forms: sweating, yawning, sneezing, laughing, yelling, crying, and the one most people fear in ceremonies: throwing up. Many of us have negative associations with this; it is a sign of weakness or distress for the body, as purging in life can make us extraordinarily vulnerable. But in ancient cultures, the purge becomes the path to freedom. Purging during a shamanic journey can actually be a sign of self-care and much needed nurturing and love. It is a tangible expulsion of toxins, our body's innate ability to remove what is holding us back. And the purging induced by plant medicine has the ability to shake us free of our deepest, most limiting, and most harmful beliefs and expel them from our experience for good as we release and recycle them back into the cosmos.

In many ancient cultures and rituals, the purge in healing journeys represents a release and ridding of all that is holding us back—emotional, physical, and spiritual toxins that have built up—and only after we release these things can new information come in. The release—whether it be physical, emotional, or spiritual—is one of the most profound elements of the human experience. When we crave healing and growth, we will inevitably come to a place where we will not be able to go any further until we let go. A full surrender and release will be required to initiate into the next level of our awareness. I found my full release in a shamanic journey. What I thought I was going for was to receive healing and a blessing, but what I realized I needed was a full release and a deep surrender to both the dark and light aspects of self I had hidden away.

It is normal to throw up in a plant medicine ceremony, and the shamans directed us to ask what this represented after each purge. During one of the ceremonies, I felt so sick to my stomach that it felt like my insides were bruised. It was clear a purge was coming, so I raced to the bathroom to release. It was the most gut-wrenchingly painful expansion. It felt like thorns on a rose bush stabbing and ripping my throat, tearing apart my insides as it was coming up. As it expelled from my body, I immediately felt lighter, healed, and more whole. Remembering the shamans' direction,

I asked what that was, and I heard, *This is your hate and shame for self. It is time to remove it!* Unbeknownst to me, the thing holding me back more than anything else in life was my decades-long turbulent relationship with myself. I thought I loved myself, but here I was years later, hunched over in the bathroom in the middle of the Costa Rican jungle with the lingering side effects of self-hatred. For decades, I had been at war with myself. It was time to wave the white flag and surrender.

I had to energetically, physically, and emotionally release my hatred toward myself in order to receive the good things that wanted to come into my life. I didn't even know I still had hate within me, but it hides out within us all in the form of comparison, shame, distrust, insecurities, and worry. It burrows itself deep in between the cracks of our thoughts and daily actions, convincing us we are not whole and complete as we are. This is what we must release—our skewed perspective of self—in order to receive the abundant gifts from the Universe. This is an energetic lesson that works on multiple levels.

Physically, spiritually, emotionally, and mentally, what do you need to release yourself from in order to receive new insights and opportunities? Frequently perspectives, habits, patterns, people, behaviors, ideas, and ways of being need to die off in order for us to meet the newer, fuller version of ourselves. So many of us are in an internal conflict with ourselves, saying yes when we want to say no, not speaking up when we have something to say, etc.

A war against yourself is essentially a war against God.

A COURSE IN MIRACLES

For decades, I believed in my ego's version of myself—the one that said you aren't pretty enough, thin enough, healthy enough, successful enough, good enough, etc. The war was vicious, but it was what I knew. But even so, I had been on a personal growth journey for decades, so I was well aware that this was the ego and not my true self. For any of us on a personal growth journey, we become aware of the ego and its attempts to hijack our well-being. But the deception is often still there, so it becomes about diving deeper into the patterns that have been created because of this ego projection.

> Your task is not to seek for love, but merely to seek and find all
> the barriers within yourself that you have built against it.
>
> RUMI

All of us have emotional and physical patterns—often in the form of self-sabotage—that drive our actions. And if you've been on a healing journey for a while, then you know it isn't about simply recognizing these limitations. That's only the beginning. It is the releasing of the darkness that is attached to those limitations. The shadows that live within us need more light. This is not to say you are wounded, broken, damaged, bad, or off track. It is simply the revelation that we can coexist with both ego and love, dark and light, and fear and faith—and this awareness can free you from emotional distress.

In order to feel better, we can start by releasing our attachment to drama. We can do this by uncovering what was previously hidden. The truth is, humans tend to gravitate toward drama. For years I found myself in dramatic situations. It seemed I was always entangled in someone's business, trying to help them through sticky situations. I would always think, *I hate drama. Why does it follow me everywhere?* But then it occurred to me that the thing all of these dramatic situations and relationships had in common was me! I was the one attracting them. And as long as I was hooked into the adrenaline of drama, I was living and leading life from my head.

LIFE TRUTH: YOUR HEART KNOWS WHAT IS TRUE.

In *A Course in Miracles*, Chapter 23, the Laws of Chaos teaches that "The purpose of chaos is to attack truth. Yet no one wants the madness, but what protects the madness is the belief that it is true." You don't have to participate and believe in the madness and chaos happening out in the world, or even the madness and chaos within yourself. It is always trying to distract you from what is real—the love and light within you—as drama and chaos are master manipulators. Their energy is a vortex of frustration, which keeps us detached from our truth. They feed off our insecurities. But your Divine Truth and inner knowing will lead you forward.

So how do we move forward in times of chaos and confusion? Ask yourself, how do you feel? Do you feel frustrated, confused, overwhelmed, and exhausted? If so, this is a sure sign you've been directing your attention to the madness and illusions of both your inner and outer worlds. This means that the ego has been in control, leading you into deeper darkness. Spiritual wisdom shows that the ego will dissolve itself, and when it does, truth comes to light.

On the flip side, the parts of you controlled by ego will be removed with more nurturing love and light. Maybe you feel empowered, alive, connected, and purpose driven? If so, this is your indication of a connection to love over fear. Since everything in the world is a matter of choice, you can choose to feel better now. Your insecurities, habits, and shadow sides do not have to define or limit you. The way forward is through the narrow passage of truth and light. You can choose to be the light in an often-dark world, and you can choose to live from your heart in what often feels like a heartless world—and in doing this, you can free yourself from the confines of the world. You do this by refusing to participate in the chaos and drama of the world. Instead, shine your own light on the dark dimensions of your inner world so you can heal and transform. As you actively participate more in your own healing journey, you start to see what is real and what is illusion parading around as fear.

LIFE TRUTH: TO HEAL, WE REVEAL WHAT IS READY TO BE SEEN IN THE LIGHT.

If we are honest, we are all at war with ourselves on some level. As we live in a world of such chaos, the contrast presented fuels this inner dialogue and back-and-forth. We aren't born hating ourselves and resisting life; we learn it. The war with self is given to us by society, systems, programming, and ancestral karma. Our parents unknowingly pass beliefs down to us, or we witness injustices and trauma out in the world, and we want to do more, but we feel hopeless. The war wears many hats. Although the outside world may seem chaotic, it is actually our inner world that is usually in the most chaos. I've come to learn that the battle all of us are really fighting is the war within ourselves. It's the battle that says:

- I want to follow my heart, but I don't want to fail.
- I want to express myself, but I worry I won't fit in.
- I want to do more to help those in need, but I feel helpless.
- Who am I to go after what I love when others are suffering?
- I don't feel safe, but I will pretend everything is okay.
- I am ashamed of how I look, so I will hide myself from the world.
- I don't want to be a burden, so I will stay quiet.
- I want to eat what I love, but it's considered bad for me.
- I can't slow down. I need to prove myself, but I am exhausted.
- I hate being in control of everything, but if I let go, I feel I won't be safe.
- I have an opinion I want to share, but what if no one understands me?

The list of endless internal battles continues. We are all in a constant push-pull, fight or flight, good versus bad relationship within our own self. We need to release the war against ourselves in order to receive Divine Love.

The biggest battle I faced for decades was the battle against my own body. Our relationship with our body can say a lot about our beliefs. As Louise Hay shares in *You Can Heal Your Life*, "The body, like everything else in life, is a mirror of our inner thoughts and beliefs. The body is always talking to us, if we will only take the time to listen. Every cell within your body responds to every single thought you think and every word you speak."[24]

Many of us look at our body from the human perspective rather than the spiritual perspective. Our higher self knows that our body is a home for our spirit and a place to be nurtured, loved, and supported. But from a human perspective, oftentimes our bodies put limitations on us, and freedom is not possible when we perceive ourselves as our body. Another block keeping us from genuine inner peace is that we

---

24   Louise Hay, *You Can Heal Your Life* (New York: Hay House, 1984), 123.

think we are our bodies, but we are not. Our bodies are an expression, a sanctuary, a vessel, and a home for our spirit. Lesson 199 of *A Course in Miracles* says, "And the only purpose of the body is the one given to it by the mind as a teaching device for learning how to awaken from all illusions separating us from love." It also says, "I am not a body. I am free. The body is the ego's chosen home, it is an image we have of ourselves outside of ourselves." Our bodies are part of the mask, the persona, the disguise. Not knowing our true identities, which extend far beyond the body, we think of ourselves as bodies, which limits us. But the body is neither good nor bad. It is a temporary limitation in form. Freeing ourselves from the idea that we are our bodies connects us to a greater truth and deeper awareness of our true nature.

LIFE TRUTH: WE ARE EXPANSIVE BEINGS AND AN EXPRESSION OF INFINITE DIVINE LIGHT.

Trapping ourselves in the belief that we are our bodies keeps us locked into a paradigm of not feeling good enough. We live in a society that focuses a lot on the physical in what often feels like a superficial way. We talk about, think about, worry about our bodies' physical appearance—how they look, how much they weigh, how healthy they are, what others think of them, etc. It is a constant focus of the already tired and exhausted human brain. We overthink our appearances and wonder if our bodies are enough, but in this constant push-pull, we are at war with our true self. Our spiritual self is so much bigger than our body and has no limitations. To the spirit, the body is beautiful, no matter what. But we forget this as we strive to make our bodies fit and perfect, yet in doing so, we take attention away from nurturing and caring for our whole self. Your whole self is what wants more attention and care.

Steve Sisgold, the author of *What's Your Body Telling You?* shares that we can tap into the power of "whole body consciousness" and use the innate wisdom of our bodies to reduce stress, create peace, and attract success in our lives. This means the number on the scale does not determine your worth. Your level of health (or lack thereof) is not an indication of your value as a human being. Your gray hair starting to show, or your lack of hair, or whatever other physical issue you obsess about doesn't matter. We are so much more than our body. Think about what you could do with all the time you spend obsessing over how to change your looks or make yourself more likable.

One of the teachings that helped me detach from thinking I'm my body is the concept of Ten Light Bodies of Consciousness from Kundalini Yoga. In *The Aquarian Teacher Level One Instructor Yoga Manual,* Yogi Bhajan shares the power of each light body. We have one physical body, three mental bodies, and six energy bodies.

The bodies are:

- First Body—Soul Body
- Second Body—Negative Mind
- Third Body—Positive Mind
- Fourth Body—Neutral Mind
- Fifth Body—Physical Body
- Sixth Body—Arcline
- Seventh Body—Aura
- Eighth Body—Pranic Body
- Ninth Body—Subtle Body
- Tenth Body—Radiant Body

The foundation of this teaching is, "If you understand that you are Ten Bodies, and you are aware of those Ten Bodies, and you keep them in balance, the whole universe will be in balance with you."[25]

> The physical body is the form that houses the soul, through which enlightenment and service to humanity can be created.
>
> YOGI BHAJAN

---

25 Sierra Hollister, "Kundalini Sequence to Awaken the Ten Bodies," *Yoga Journal,* March 23, 2018, yogajournal.com/yoga-101/kundalini-sequence-to-awaken-the-10-bodies/.

When we realize that our physical body is a vehicle through which all aspects of ourselves can exist and find expression, then we can release our limited view of attaching ourselves to the body. When our physical body is out of balance, we feel weak, angry, jealous, greedy, fatigued, and ungrateful, and we are susceptible to illness. As Kundalini teaching shares, when the body is overly connected to the ego, it turns into an obsession with physical appearance, physical abilities, and the material world. To feel more harmonious with your physical body, develop a routine that keeps the body strong and flexible. Extend your energy to elevate others by being grounded in your own light and love. This will help to support the health of your body, mind, and spirit. As Yogi Bhajan says, "When the God in you and the human in you are in parallel consciousness, then you are in harmony. You have no duality, you have Divine vision, and the truth flows from you." You don't have to find anything outside of you. If this feels a bit heady or esoteric, no worries—just know that whole-body consciousness is a powerful way to reclaim your power by bringing your awareness back to your true nature.

This concept, in part, helped my body return to its optimal balance. After decades of struggling with my weight and being at war with myself and my body, I applied the concepts from this lesson to myself. I saw that my added body weight was a manifestation of my own self-judgment and of my ego trying to fixate on my body image and always wanting to change it. By understanding that I am not my body, but that my body is actually a home for my spirit, I was able to release judgments, shame, and self-blame. Through a dedication to wanting to be healthier and more whole within myself, I started a daily routine of implementing all the lessons in this book, along with a meditation to practice and align with the concepts of whole-body consciousness (which I share on the next page), and I've lost over forty pounds so far.

Whole-body consciousness is realizing we are not our bodies, and in this perspective, we are free. To help release our attachment to the body, we can lean on Lesson 209 in *A Course in Miracles*:

A Prayer for Releasing Your Attachment to the Body

I am not a body. I am free. For I am still as God created me. I feel the Love of God within me now. The Love of God is what created me. The Love of God is everything I am . . . The Love of God within me sets me free.

Here's another meditation you can to do help align your light bodies and practice whole-body consciousness.

Vibrational Healing Meditation for Body Peace

Repeat these words: "Dear Universal support system of
love and light, please remove all negative energy, thoughts,
and perceptions directed at me or within me."
Next, visualize the energy of your higher self as a most glorious
golden-white light pouring in through the top of your head.
Picture the white crystalized light flooding your entire
body with warm, loving presence and flushing through
your whole being. As the light touches each cell, it
transforms it into pure health and ultimate vibrancy.
See the white light soothing all of your cells
and activating their highest potential.
Feel the energy flush through you as it transforms
all disharmony and discomfort.
Repeat these words aloud three times: "I
acknowledge the light within me. I accept the
perfect love that I am. I am whole. I am love."

Love created me like itself.

A COURSE IN MIRACLES

When we align with this sacred truth, we realize we are birthed from love, and love is our serenity and where our safety lies. Love is the voice of truth, and when we align with it, the ego and everything it tells us about ourselves is replaced with one simple truth: you were created by love itself. Take a moment to really feel the power of this notion, and bask in the love that you are. Release all the ego projections, and allow yourself to receive the true nature of your magnificence. When we realize, remember, and live from this awareness, we step into a deeper experience of life, one that is richer and more whole. We reclaim our power, and we are able to receive the gifts available to us in being alive. No longer do we allow the outside world to dictate how our bodies should look, but we instead bring forth the innate wisdom from our true selves that our bodies are beautiful (no matter what size, shape, color, health condition, etc.) because they are our souls' chosen home.

Once I started to see my body as a home for my spirit, I stopped attacking it with negative words and energy. I started to nurture it and listen to its guidance. I felt guided to take better care of it and send it kind thoughts. By building a relationship with my body, my life felt more manageable, and I returned to love. As I prioritized self-love and care, my connection to both myself and Spirit grew stronger. As this love increased, I became more balanced and present for those around me. The biggest battle I needed to overcome in my life wasn't depression, eating disorders, or drug addiction. Those were all manifestations of the deep-seated fears driving my every move. Those were all side effects of my imbalanced perspective that we live in an unsafe world and I am not safe to be who I am. The war within myself wasn't that I hated my body or blamed it for my shortcomings. But the constant conflict within me had become a relationship where I was always on guard because I felt unsafe in our world.

The most important decision we make is whether we
believe we live in a friendly or hostile universe.

ALBERT EINSTEIN

If you believe we live in a hostile world, your inner world will be a battlefield. As you fight, resist, and push against what is, you exhaust yourself in the expression of living. But if you see the world as a friendly place—one of abundance, joy, opportunity, and love—you will feel safer, and in this safety, your peace and security lie. We are always living in duality and have the option to live in one of two worlds: one of fear and hostility or one of love and friendliness. When we feel safe, we are creative, and we're able to express ourselves; we are choosing to live in the friendly Universe. But when we are in angst, worry, or fear, we are choosing to see the world through the lens of hostility. Our war against the world and our war within ourselves are about safety. Do you feel safe in this world? Safe to be who you really are—safe to be seen, heard, expressed, acknowledged, understood? The manifestation of all of our imbalances comes back down to a fundamental human need: safety. This is why the invitation to explore more deeply into the shadow sides of our life, look at where we feel unsafe, and bring in even more love is so important.

Love knows no bounds; love and light are within you always, and your healing requires a releasing of all the burdens you carry. Our ego has convinced us that it is not a safe world. If we haven't allowed ourselves to trust the Divine or receive peace and serenity, then we can't share it. If we haven't allowed ourselves to receive love, then we can't give it. Our inability to receive blocks us from feeling inner peace.

We must first be willing to receive. Only then can we release. This means we need to learn how to accept and acknowledge our discomforts. Most of us have a difficult time receiving. The inability to receive support from others is a trauma response, which can show up in many forms. For me, it was in my fierce and fabulous independent nature. For the past several years, I have focused solely on my career and avoided serious romantic relationships, going on a few dates here and there but never allowing myself to get too serious. I didn't realize until I started dating more seriously again that I needed to go deeper into my inner shadows to reveal that my "I don't need anyone; I am happy on my own" conditioning is actually a survival tactic. Many of us have this wildly independent streak, which is a protective mechanism and trauma response.

It looks like this:

- I don't need anyone. I will just do it myself.
- I don't want to burden others with my situation, ideas, troubles, etc.
- I can't count on anyone.
- I feel taken for granted.
- I am not supported.
- No one understands me. I am alone.
- The only way something will get done is if I do it myself.
- I'm always there for others, but no one is there for me.

Jamila White, a psychic and life coach, shared her perspective on this in a Facebook post that went viral. She talks about trauma responses and how they play out in our life.

She wrote:

> *The inability to receive support from others is a trauma response. Your "I don't need anyone, I'll just do it all myself" conditioning is a survival tactic. You needed it to shield your tender heart from abuse, neglect, betrayal, and disappointment from those who could not or would not be there for you.*
>
> *From the parent who was absent by choice or by the circumstance of working three jobs to feed and house you.*
>
> *From the lovers who offered sexual intimacy but offered no safe haven that honored your heart.*
>
> *From the friendships that always took more than they gave.*
>
> *From all the situations when someone told you "we're in this together" then abandoned you, leaving you to pick up the pieces when shit got real, leaving you to handle your part and their part, too.*
>
> *From the lies. The betrayals.*
>
> *You learned along the way that you just couldn't really trust people. Or that you could trust people, but only up to a certain point.*
>
> *Ultra-independence is a "trust issue."*[26]

---

26   Jamila White (@InspiredJamila), Facebook post, September 15, 2020, m.facebook.com/InspiredJamila/photos/a.543152759084556/3498211960245273/?type=3&source=48.

We learn how to behave through our shared experiences. And one of the biggest wars within our own minds is the deception that we don't need anyone. We believe the lies we tell ourselves. And for me, these lies turned into a decade of self-sabotage and emotional pain that manifested into unhealthy patterns of isolation, emotional eating, and control. By ignoring my deepest desires for intimacy and support, I pretended everything was okay. We are the great pretenders; so many of us wear masks as we pretend to fit the role of what we think we need to be. But to truly move forward into grace, we need to love ourselves by turning the shadows into light. How do we do this? We address them; we look at them head on, without judgment or shame, but with compassion and love. Healing requires a release of the burdens you've cast upon yourself. Ultimately, it comes down to this: forgiveness. Forgive yourself by loving and accepting all of you. The barriers you have within you keep you distracted and distant from the world. You can release the fear that you are not safe to be who you truly are.

Our war with our self shows up in a myriad of ways. Maybe you don't feel fiercely independent, but you don't feel safe to be who you really are. Perhaps you find yourself always in a relationship, one after another, and you can't recall the last time you were alone. This can also be a protection mechanism and trauma response. Whether it is not relying on others (as in "If I don't put myself in a situation where I rely on someone, I won't have to be disappointed"); or you don't trust yourself to choose people; or "I need to be with someone to feel safe, and I don't trust myself to be alone"; it all comes back to the trauma response of not feeling safe nor trusting the world in which we live. If we don't feel safe in this world, then we won't feel safe to be ourselves. This means we are not trusting ourselves or the Universe. We are acting from a place of protection, which is a sure sign the ego is in control.

While writing this book, the team for Martha Beck, who is one of my favorite authors and Oprah's life coach, reached out to me to endorse her new book that was coming out called *The Way of Integrity*. As I was reading through an advance copy of the book, there was a section that really stood out to me, a chapter titled "The End of Self-Betrayal." In it, she shares that the lies we tell ourselves are key to creating space for a breakthrough. Start by simply noticing occasions when you cheat, lie to, and betray yourself. It's important to know that you may be doing these things to others as well, but it's absolutely crucial to see where you're doing them to yourself.

> *Everything is easy once you believe your own lies. When we deliberately leave our own truth, we live in a foggy world where nothing we experience feels trustworthy or reliable, because we ourselves aren't trustworthy and reliable. The goal then is to build back trust with yourself and we do this by being honest with ourselves. Maya Angelou wrote, "Courage is the most important of all the virtues, because without courage you can't practice any other virtue consistently." Lying is the dark counterpart to courage: it's the most important of all the vices, because without lying you can't practice any other vice consistently (if you never lie, your ego plots just won't pan out). Conversely, if you can't stop lying—at least to yourself—you'll never make it out of the inferno.*[27]

To heal this pattern, we must abide in radical trust. To trust is to hope; to trust is to be vulnerable. No matter how we dress it up and proudly display our life to make it seem like we are okay and everything is fine, in truth it's just our wounded, scared, broken heart behind a protective brick wall. And trusting means breaking down the internal prison we've placed ourselves in.

The war we are all fighting is a silent battle within our own mind, against ourselves. We build an impenetrable fortress. No hurt gets in, but no love gets in either. Fortresses and armor are for those in battle, or who believe the battle is coming. Every single one of us has built some type of protection around ourselves. The walls and masks inevitably keep love away. This is a trauma response.

---

27   Martha Beck, *The Way of Integrity* (New York: The Open Field, 2021), 130.

*The good news is trauma that is acknowledged is
trauma that can be healed.*

You are worthy of having support.
You are worthy of having true partnership.
You are worthy of love.
You are worthy of having your heart held.
You are worthy to be adored.
You are worthy to be cherished.

You are worthy to have someone say, "You rest. I got this."
And actually deliver on that promise.

You don't have to earn it.
You don't have to prove it.
You don't have to bargain for it.
You don't have to beg for it.

You are worthy.
Worthy.

Simply because you exist.[28]

---

28   Jamila White (@InspiredJamila), Facebook post, September 15, 2020, m.facebook.com
/InspiredJamila/photos/a.543152759084556/3498211960245273/?type=3&source=48.

You can repeat this mantra by Monika Muranyi: "I am willing to accept the perfect love of the Creator." Repeating this mantra daily will help you shake down the walls that have been built up around your heart. When we stop pushing, trying, controlling, manipulating, resisting, arguing, and fighting against the world and ourselves, we can relax into the moment and allow ourselves to be. When we rest in the moment, silence steps in. In the space of silence is truth. Give yourselves permission to receive love—love from the prime Creator, Divine Love; love to ourselves from ourselves—and make light from the world your focus. When we commit to staying open to love, even in the face of our own pain or when we want to shut down, we see in this moment that we are safe and there is nothing to be afraid of, ever, for love is the true protector and where our safety lies.

Take five minutes every day to receive the love available to you. You can do this by releasing the need to control your outcomes or protect yourself from a world that feels scary. When you live your life from love and from your heart, you are protected and can seek solace in the light. You see that your ego could never give you the safety you searched for; only Divine Love provides true protection. Instead of seeking to armor yourself, step into a place of being the "receiver." It is much harder than giving. It can be risky, as it makes us vulnerable. Most of us on a personal growth path don't know how to properly receive, so we end up over-giving. But in order to truly feel balance and alignment with our own inner light, we must be willing to release the constant battle within our own self and against the world. We do this by receiving the love available to us and within us. It's safe to relax into life and let your emotional guard down. You can commit to keeping your heart open. Accept that you are love, you are worthy of love, and you are here to be and experience the layers of love. Be willing to accept the perfect love of the Creator, and express this in all you do.

Let's put this lesson into practice:

To apply this lesson, In Order to Receive, You Must Release, try these steps.

Step 1: Bring your shadows into the light.
When we commit to living a life of peace, we are led to integrity and truth. And this focus will reveal all the ways in which we have played it safe and stayed small. When we believe our insecurities and the lies we tell about ourselves, they keep us trapped in a small but predictable reality, forcing us to hide our light. But your mission and soul work are to shine your light and rise above the darkness. When we recognize our habits and projections as illusions holding us back, we can release their influence and choose to live in our light. There is a hidden power within us; it's called authenticity. It's called your unique self, your true nature. The light within you is so immense, and when you see that your ego is attempting to hijack your true safety, the light and love will emerge, and your true self will shine.

Step 2: Listen to and love your body.
A Course in Miracles says, "Freedom must be impossible as long as you perceive a body as yourself." But our bodies are merely images we have of ourselves that are outside of ourselves. When we identify with our body and make it good or bad, we distort the truth—that our body is only temporary but our spirit is eternal. By hooking into the ego's projection that our bodies being who we are, we use it as yet another mask to keep love away. We think we are our bodies, but these bodies are vessels for growth. The body itself is neither good nor bad; just like the world we live in, the body itself is neutral. Your body is designed to help free you from your ego projections. To aid in this process, you can repeat this mantra from Lesson 84 in *A Course in Miracles*: "I am in the likeness of my Creator. I cannot suffer, I cannot experience loss, and I cannot die. I am not a body . . . I am in the likeness of my Creator. Love created me like itself."

Step 3: Release so you can receive.

When you look at all areas of your life and ask yourself what no longer feels in alignment, you will start to see the imbalances that can no longer be ignored. It can be terrifying to let go of aspects of your life, but it is necessary for your optimal growth. Holding on will only keep you stuck in a static, unfulfilling routine. When we hold on to what wants to be released, we are resisting the natural flow of life. Shifts are happening all around you. Think of it as spring cleaning for your soul. Be clear and intentional about what you will no longer allow in your life. Negative and self-sabotaging thinking, doubt, and drama are all available by choice. We give consent to all things in our life. If there is an area you are not satisfied with and feel overwhelmed by, focus on your intention to feel peace, and align with what feels better. As you do, you open yourself up to more abundance, love, and appreciation. The Universe has a beautiful plan for you, but you must let go of the attachments, ego projections, and your inner critic in order to welcome in a more peaceful experience.

As you step away from what no longer serves you, you are being asked to shatter illusions of separation, which is why you may feel as if so, so much is crumbling around you. Use this time to reflect and realign. Go inward, and really get clear about who you are, what you stand for, and what matters most to you. Do you stand in the light, or is fear your comforter? When you are aligned with the truth, you have nothing to fear. Keep your head high, and know that your world is always shifting into more love.

Step 4: Wave the white flag and surrender the war within yourself.

You are so magnificent and perfect just as you are. We put so much pressure on ourselves to be more, do more, and have more, which prevents us from seeing our true light. Commit to being your own best friend. Stand proud in your truth, and let go of the negative thoughts holding you back. Release the constant battle and conflicts within by accepting yourself and allowing yourself to open up and receive love.

Questions to ask:

1. How can I build a more positive relationship with my body and listen to and understand more of its needs?

2. What battle within myself am I committed to healing?

3. Do I believe we live in a hostile or friendly Universe?

4. What do I want to release?

5. What am I ready to receive?

Once we understand that the real troubles, conflicts, and frustrations are not outside of us out in the world, but within, we can release them. By applying the steps in this lesson, we learn to drop the walls we've built up under the illusion of creating safety and can now allow ourselves to receive love. In the next lesson, you will learn how to trust yourself more by tapping into synchronicity and universal life flow. You'll discover how the Universe is always working in Divine Order to support whatever is for your highest good.

LESSON 9

THE UNIVERSE
REWARDS MOTION

A couple of years ago, I spoke at a wellness conference in Canada. I was giving one of my signature talks on how to believe and trust in yourself, which I had given dozens of times before. It is a powerful lecture that usually resonates well with audiences, but this day was different. As I stood on stage and shared the principles, something felt off. No one was laughing at my regular jokes; no one was taking notes; not one soul wanted to participate in the shared group activities, which were an integral part of the workshop; and no one was giving me any feedback at all, whatsoever. I was looking out at hundreds of stoic faces, and I felt like a deer in the headlights. I started to disconnect from the teaching and began a running internal dialogue. I was stuck in my head, overanalyzing and criticizing myself. I wondered why my information was not being well received, and my inner critic took the opportunity to tell me everything that was wrong with me and the situation, claiming things like, "After almost eight years of lecturing, I am still not good enough and no one cares about what I have to say." The frustration took over, and I broke out into a cold sweat. I found myself speeding through the material just to get past the pain and torture of being so uncomfortable. I felt like one of those cartoon characters on stage who was bombing their act, anticipating the giant hook to come out and swipe them away. Anything to end this embarrassment.

Finally, I wrapped it up, ending almost ten minutes early, and said thank you. As I wiped the sweat from my brow, I looked up and was totally surprised. People were standing up, cheering and clapping as fast as they could. One after another, they popped out of their seats to share their enthusiasm for my presentation. It was the first standing ovation I'd ever received and one of the loudest cheers I had heard from any keynote I'd given. Some women were crying and even pulled me aside afterward to thank me for such a powerful talk.

I was so perplexed. How could I have interpreted the situation so differently? I thought I was bombing it, but in fact, this was one of the most well-received talks I'd ever given, though I had no idea while I was giving it. I was looking for the audience to let me know I was doing well (aka external feedback), and my ego took the opportunity to jump in and try to convince me that I was failing miserably. Even after years of being a professional speaker and doing my soul mission work, my inner critic was able to get the better of me.

Our ego will take every chance it can to try to convince us that we are not doing this life thing right. That we are somehow messing up, that we are stupid, that we don't belong, that our dreams don't matter, and that we should just quit. But this is merely smoke and mirrors, as it is yet another ego manipulation to try to dim our light and block us from seeing our own brilliant power.

Ironically, the talk I was giving at this conference was on believing and trusting in yourself, yet when I didn't have feedback from the outside world, I started to second-guess myself. This is classic human behavior, as we naturally look for feedback and reassurance. Many of us need recognition in order to stay on our path and continue to move forward. But this is counterproductive to the laws of the Universe, the guiding lesson being that the Universe rewards motion, and the more inspired action steps you take, the more the Universe can support you. This habit of looking to others for approval only keeps us from establishing a stronger connection to our true self. I was looking for others to give me validation that I was on track and doing a good job, but our true self is already enough and does not need any form of outside approval, especially when we are connected to Source Energy.

During my talk, the one thing I didn't do was reach out for spiritual support. In that moment of overwhelm onstage, I could have paused, turned inward, and instead of panicking accessed peace. I could have reached for my higher self and higher power, and connected to Source Energy and the infinite field of love and light. By tapping into this pool of energic resonance, I would have realigned myself. But I didn't know about the power of the field then. At that time, I didn't have a strong connection to self or to Spirit, so instead, I ended up with cold sweats and a mini panic attack.

Do you find yourself stuck in doubt or worry or needing approval or feedback from the outside world to determine your worth? You're not alone. In my workshops and client sessions, one of the biggest barriers to peace is not believing or trusting ourselves. And when we don't trust ourselves, we look outside of ourselves for validation—all the while not realizing that we are the love and faith we seek and what we are looking for is already within us. It is our inner knowing that can lead us forward and connect us to the God-light and love within. But when we are stuck in doubt and worried about what others think, we stay trapped under the ego's control. When we can abandon our doubts, we will strip away our need for outside influence. This allows us to feel better by connecting to higher frequencies of acceptance, love, and peace.

How do you move from doubt and turn it into confidence? With faith in yourself, which means you truly understand and recognize how unique, special, and sacred you are by taking physical action to move towards your goals. The more inspired action steps we take, the more confidence we build, and the more we align with our true self and honor a deeper connection to the Universe.

LIFE TRUTH: YOU'RE IN A DIVINE PARTNERSHIP WITH THE UNIVERSE, WHERE YOU'LL ALWAYS CO-CREATE THE OUTCOME THAT IS FOR THE HIGHEST GOOD OF ALL INVOLVED.

One of my teachers, the late Wayne Dyer, used to demonstrate this concept with mangoes in his presentations. He would invite someone who had never tasted a mango before to be a volunteer. Then, the people in the audience who had eaten the fruit were to tell the person who had never tried it how the mango tasted. As you can imagine, frustration would ensue. Without fail, they all soon learned how pointless their attempts were. Obviously, the volunteer would always return to their seat without truly knowing how a mango tasted. The conclusion: it is impossible to convey or translate experiences and information if you haven't tried it firsthand. There was no trust or confidence in self because no mango was actually eaten.

You see where we are going, right? This is the same idea as having self-doubt when we need faith in ourselves. We can try to lean on others outside of ourselves for "validation," "approval," or "feedback," but it can never sustain us the way our inner faith or knowing will. We build up our inner faith muscles with experience. The more you try, the more you learn, and the more you experience, the more confidence you gain in your own abilities. But here is the sneaky truth that no one really talks about: even when you have a ton of experience, you may still have moments of uncertainty. I certainly did. I had been speaking for years, yet doubt found a way to creep in. The way through these blocks of uncertainty, doubt, and fear is with faith and trust in yourself and the Universe. We can grow our connection to our true self and gain more confidence through action. We do this by connecting to the universal field (also known as "the Field") of energy that is supportive and benevolent. The field is all the energy of abundant love, and it is full of information.

The Tao teaches the power of the infinite field that connects us to Source. It also teaches that our blockages in life stem from negative information we store in our minds and bodies, based often on painful past experiences. So the goal is to connect to the field to get more information, and when we have this new information, we can transmute the negative energy into a more positive focus. This process can also bring us closer to our true self.

What this means is that anytime you feel stuck or in doubt, shame, or blame, you just need more information. Since information comes with experience, when you find yourself feeling uncertainty, take guided action, which will give you more insight and help you step into alignment with your actualized self.

LIFE TRUTH: THE WAY TO IS ALWAYS THROUGH.

We live in a Universe that supports intention and action. It often shows up in the form of synchronicity. Maybe you've experienced *synchronicity* recently, such as thinking about an old friend you haven't talked to in years, and they call or text; or you start daydreaming about a new job, and before you even start to look, you receive a job offer through a friend; or maybe you are running late for an important appointment, and all the traffic lights stay green, and traffic seems to move out of your way. Regardless of your own beliefs, background, or habits, synchronicity happens all the time and is available to help guide you forward to live with more ease, comfort, and peace.

I lived in this Divine flow one weekend when I went to an intuition workshop in Arizona with Lee Carroll and Marilyn Harper (who work with Kryon and Adironnda, respectively). During one of the breaks, my intuition said to go up to the teachers and say hi. I didn't know what I wanted to ask or why I was going up to them, aside from thanking them for putting the event together and doing the work they do. But as I shook their hands in gratitude, I found my inner voice speaking for me. I asked, "What suggestions do you have for best expanding my spiritual connection and developing my intuition?" Without skipping a beat, Lee Carroll said, "Are you coming to the intuition and energetic healing workshop on Monday?" I said, "Yes, I am already signed up." And he said, "Great, start there."

When Monday came, I was excited for the full-day workshop on how to channel and grow my intuition. But I had no idea how in the flow and synchronistic the day would actually turn out to be. To start the morning, the teachers said to the group, "Whose birthday is March 11?" I raised my hand, not sure why they had called my birthday. They said, "Congratulations, you just won this gift set," which included a special intention-setting water bottle and energy cards. I thought to myself, *Wow, I have never won anything like this before. How cool!* As we dove into the workshop, more synchronicities occurred. I sat next to a woman who was in the process of writing her own book, and when she found out that I was an author mentor, she wanted to learn about my author mentorship programs and has since become a client and dear friend of mine.

By midday, I was feeling really good and buzzing from all the synchronicities that had occurred. At lunchtime, we were told to find our nametags, which were already set up on the chairs where we were to sit. As I looked for my name, I wondered who I would spend the next hour with at lunch, and I was thrilled to see that sitting at my table was the teacher of the workshop. This meant I had an extra hour of personal time to connect with her. *What a gift from the Universe*, I thought. When she asked what I did, I told her I am an author and I write books about connecting to your true self and living with more meaning and joy. "Wait, you're Shannon Kaiser!" she replied. I was confused, not realizing that the mentor who I was there to learn from already knew of me. She said, "Your book *Joy Seeker* is my latest joy." I laughed out loud and smiled with such gratitude—my own mentor and teacher had my book. And then, when we returned to the workshop, she asked everyone what they learned on break. As she passed the microphone around, she said out loud to the entire class, "Shannon Kaiser, the author of *Joy Seeker*, is here, and I had lunch with her. Her book is on my nightstand at home," and all eyes turned around to look at me. People smiled and laughed, and as uncomfortable as it felt, I recognized that this was the Universe giving me the gift of being seen and receiving. I was living a day of pure flow—no effort, just relaxation, joy, and wonder. Pure synchronicity.

I had no expectations going into the workshop. I was just eager to learn and grow. By releasing my expectations, I was in a relaxed mindset, and from this place, I was able to attract more. By me being in this energy of Divine allowance, what was returned was recognition, love, support, respect, and abundance. The synchronicities continued throughout the entire day, including the workshop teachers asking me to email them and send some writing samples, as they were looking for some author support for their own business and books, and I later became a guest teacher for

Lee Carroll's Kryon Circle of Twelve event. I came home that day with pure gratitude and was shocked at how fun and easy the entire day had been. I simply kept an open mind and showed up with a childlike sense of wonder and curiosity, and the day unfolded beautifully, with one opportunity after another just falling into my lap. This is the way all of our lives can be when we trust the Universe and align ourselves with the loving field of Source Energy. We can trust in the strength of love and put our faith in the unknown, because the unknown is a direct link to an infinite source of abundance, love, and light. Synchronicities happen all the time. Most of the time, we need to just get out of our own way and relax, release, and allow.

Esther Hicks, who shares the wisdom of Abraham, is the queen of teaching synchronicities, calling it "the vortex": "Simply put, the vortex is a place you get to when you are in complete alignment with your inner being and the universe." The vortex itself doesn't come to you. Instead you align your energy to be a positive vibrational match, and you pop into the vortex. Think of a river flowing with good vibes, positive intentions, and ultimate outcomes for the well-being of all involved, and you just hop on your boat and float down the river with ease, grace, and joy. This is the power of co-creating with the Universe. But it is a dance and partnership, which means you don't just sit back and wait for things to happen. You must take inspired guided action yourself in order to see the results you want. Manifesting your dreams and desires can be fun and rewarding, but you have to keep moving forward and take action to see results. The key is to trust yourself and be in motion. The Universe will always reward you.

Let's put this lesson into practice:

These steps will help you implement this lesson, The Universe Rewards Motion.

Step 1: Find alignment with your inner world.
Part of living a synchronistic life and being one with the Universe is learning how to trust the unknown. One of the blocks that keeps us

from feeling peace is our desire to try and control everything. When uncertain things happen, we feel like we don't have a grip on our reality, so we will do what we can to try to stay focused and safe. But alignment comes from faith and believing in what we can't see. Put your energy into the unknown by believing in yourself and trusting the infinite love and support that lives all around you. Commit to aligning yourself with the energy of love, and watch how things transform for you. Lesson 339 in *A Course in Miracles* says, "I will receive whatever I request." We receive what we request from an energetic standpoint. But many don't realize that what they are requesting is not what they really want. It is all energetics, which means your desire has an energetic resonance to it. In order to receive what we truly want, we must energetically match that desire.

This is why you want to first find alignment within your heart and soul with what you truly want—not from a material standpoint, but energetically. You may want a book deal, to lose weight, or to get out of debt, but what is the energy behind these desires? Align with your true desire, which is the emotional resonance behind each focus. Examples of these deeper emotional resonances include the desire to express yourself creatively, to share your message, to feel loved and comfortable in your body, or to feel free and secure. When you focus on these alignments, the Universe can respond because you are now speaking the language of your soul.

Step 2: Align with your intentions, then move forward.
Next, you want to feel the inspiration from within you and take guided action towards your goal. Sometimes we act from a place of needing approval, of feeling not good enough, or of wanting to be recognized, appreciated, seen, and heard. These motivations can weaken your connection to your true self, as you are looking outside of yourself for what you hold within. Inspiration is part of your universal alignment, as it comes to you naturally and effortlessly when you connect to the field of love. Your higher self connects with you through your heart; when you listen to your heart, you can hear the wisdom from your own soul. Uncertainty transforms from a scary concept into a curious adventure

when you step into your power with confidence because you are aligned with the infinite Source. It is important not to look to others for validation, approval, or acknowledgment, but instead to focus on cultivating the confidence within. Your power is in your own hands with each action step you take. The more you commit to feeling good, the easier it will be to take action from a place of joy, wonder, and awe. You will step into a synchronistic current and connect with the abundant flow of loving energy that supports all well-being.

Step 3: Become an action activist.
It is so important to take action and focus your intentions daily. As you move in the direction of your desires, the Universe swoops in to support you. The more action steps you take, the faster you will get to where you want to go. In the first few years of running my own business as an author, speaker, and coach, I made a plan to do at least three things every day that my future self would hug me for. This was a fun experiment because I quickly saw firsthand the power of taking daily action. Soon results started to be a steady part of my experience because I was co-creating with the Universe daily. It is all a dance, and the more you show up for the experience, the more enjoyable, more graceful, and easier your experience will be.

Questions to ask:

1. How can I trust myself more?

2. What synchronicities have I experienced recently?

3. What guided action can I take today?

4. Where do I still seek validation or approval from outside sources, and how can I instead validate and approve of myself?

At this point in our journey, you may be able to see how each lesson plays into the next. As we move through the program, we approach the grand lessons and the truth of all of life. Life is a constantly unfolding, glorious adventure, and the more we learn to work with the loving energy available around us, the more rewarding and fun our journey will be. In the next chapter, we'll learn how expectations can actually hold us back and how to release them by freeing ourselves from the illusions around us so we can see all of life from a magnificent new perspective.

LESSON 10

NOTHING REAL CAN BE THREATENED

Several years ago, I went to Belize on a travel writing assignment, and I became friends with one of the Belize tourism representatives, Larry. Larry's philosophy of life is to take in as much knowledge as he can and always commit to personal growth. He reads a book a week and challenges all his friends to do the same. A couple of years ago, his region of the country was hit with devastating floods, completely destroying his entire community. The water damage also ruined his epic library of hundreds of books; his most cherished possessions, which had taken him decades to collect, were destroyed in less than twenty-four hours.

When I reached out to Larry to see how he was doing, he sent me his list of personal commandments:

1. I don't control the world around me, only how I respond.

2. Always respond with courage, temperance, wisdom, and justice.

3. Forgive. Forgive. Forgive.

So often we feel helpless when faced with difficult situations and suffering, especially when it affects those things and people we care about. Larry said, "No matter how bad it is or how bad it gets, I am going to make it through." Despite what happened, he was in good spirits, and he was sharing his commitment to growth and moving forward.

LIFE TRUTH: THERE IS NO FUTURE IN THE PAST.

We cannot more forward in life if we are living in the past or worried about what is lost or ruined or what devastation happened to us. What has happened has already happened. When we relive it in our mind, we stay stuck in a static state. To truly find peace, we must be present in the moment. We have the ability to connect to our power by realizing in each moment that we are always okay. It is the mind that tells us different. My friend proved that even when unexpected things happen and we feel as if the world is crashing in on us, nothing real can truly be threatened.

"Nothing real can be threatened. Nothing unreal exists. Herein lies the peace of God" is my favorite passage from the introduction of *A Course in Miracles*, as it's a Divine reminder that the most important things in life are not the "things." At times, life can feel out of control and overwhelming, but when you remind yourself where your true power lies—your connection to Source Energy and Divine Love—all illusions fall away. The love within you can pull you into a more peaceful state. When you look outside of yourself, you can easily fall into worry and feel hopeless, but your inner world is where you truly live—for your inner world is your soul and spirit. The world within you is a beautiful place where all possibilities can manifest. It always starts with you. Fear and doubt will try to threaten your well-being, but love cannot be threatened. When you are aligned with your truth, you are made from the love of the Divine Creator, and nothing can harm you.

We see this demonstrated in near-death experiences. A near-death experience, or NDE, is a profound psychological event that can occur to a person who is either close to death or in extreme physical or emotional crisis. Many report the emotions experienced during an NDE as intense, and they most commonly include peace, love, and bliss. Most people come away from the experience with an unshakable belief that they have learned something of immeasurable importance about the purpose of life and the truth of it all. According to the Near Death Experience Research Foundation (NDERF), which has amassed thousands of near-death experience stories, most return from the brink with a profound understanding of God's love. And not God in the religious sense, but in a benevolent, eternal sense. Even if they were unaware of its origin, many reported an absolute feeling of love and light. While the concept of God can be a convoluted topic, since you've made it this far into the book, you've noticed me use multiple terms to refer to God. The way I see it is, God isn't a person or thing but an experience and energy. The ancient Latin manuscript called the *Book of the Twenty-Four Philosophers* shares a useful perspective: "God is an infinite sphere whose center is everywhere and whose circumference is nowhere."[29] Which means the center of everything is love, and love is everywhere. It all comes back to you, as you are the center of your own universe, and everything you live is created through you. In this context, everything else is an illusion that separates you from the Divine Truth that you are from the Creator, Source Energy, and love is what and who you are. It is no surprise this type of love is always felt when people have near-death experiences.

Some say:

"Love was everywhere. It permeated the afterlife. It was incredible."

"This was a being so pure and so benevolent and so non-judgmental I could barely comprehend the level of compassion this being possessed in the small yet brilliant light that it was."

"I knew that love was the greatest force around us and that we are all love, and love is the only thing that is real, that hatred and pain and hurt and all the negative things are not really the way it is, that we just create these negative thoughts."

---

29   Anonymous, from Latin manuscript called the *Book of the Twenty-Four Philosophers*.

"The peace, the love and serenity that I felt was like nothing I ever felt, and I wanted to stay there enjoying that wonderful feeling." [30]

One very common element of an NDE is that those who go through the experience report feeling as if the place they went to was more loving, kinder, and more real than anything they'd ever experienced before. Furthermore, their perspectives forever change as they learn that love is real and it can never be threatened. It is the one thing that is everlasting and real. When people return from this experience, their old worries, concerns, and fears fall away. Many of the people who go through these experiences say they didn't want to come back because they had exposure to the truth of who they really are, and it was astonishing. Truth revealed itself, and they could never go back to the illusions.

LIFE TRUTH: TO ACCESS TRUE PEACE, WE MUST KNOW WHAT IS REAL AND UNREAL.

We must make a fundamental distinction between knowledge and perception. This lesson is an invitation to see the world with fresh eyes—the real world of love, compassion, joy—and participate in the activation of heaven on earth. The world in which we live is, in part, an illusion. It is not real in the sense that we give such importance to things outside of ourselves that don't really matter. The material things—the likes, the follows, the outward forms of success—are not representative of your true worth. They are all fictions created to pull you away from the image of love within you. Things outside of you can be manipulated reality, but the real world is the one in your heart. The intangibles of hope, peace, joy, and love—these are your true power, the part of you that is your spirit and soul.

---

30   Near-Death Experience Research Foundation (NDERF), "Archive List," accessed November 18, 2020, nderf.org/Archives/archivelist.htm.

LIFE TRUTH: WHEN YOU ALIGN WITH WHAT IS REAL, YOU STEP INTO PURE PEACE.

As humans, we tend to see things through a scarcity mindset. This is the illusion of separation we elect to take part in as a life assignment so we can attempt to remove it. The scarcity concept governs the whole world of illusions. As *A Course in Miracles* mentions in its preface, "It is the Holy Spirit's goal to help us escape from the dream world by teaching us how to reverse our thinking." The goal is to truly awaken within our own dream state and see that we have always been the dreamer within our own dream.

My friend Summer Bacon described this in such a tangible way. Get ready for your mind to be blown (mine certainly was when I first was introduced to this concept by her). She said, "Imagine going to sleep one night, and the same way you have dreams and go into a deep, restful, altered state, you wake up and feel refreshed and say, 'Wow, what a great night's sleep. What an interesting dream I just had.' This is the same idea of our life here on Earth. But you are in a waking dream; our life is an experiment, a giant adventure, and it goes by fast. You will wake up on the other side and look at your life on Earth the same way: 'Wow, what a crazy dream that was!'" You know the famous childhood song, "Row, Row, Row Your Boat"? The lyrics go "Gently down the stream / Merrily, merrily, merrily, merrily / Life is but a dream." There is truth to this. What we call *death* is actually an awakening to your truth—the eternal spirit of love that you are. Once we realize that our life is like a dream, and it is but a short speck of time, we get to participate in it more fluidly and fully, without being attached to any specific outcome. We free ourselves from the confines of the system.

This lesson is about dissolving the biggest illusion of all—separation from Source, which is the dream state we function in. But how do we let go of an illusion if we don't know we are in one?

You are the dreamer of the world of dreams.

A COURSE IN MIRACLES

As *A Course in Miracles* Chapter 27 teaches, "No one can waken from a dream the world is dreaming for him." Most of us are alive, but we are not really living. We live in a society that invites suboptimal function, such as eating overly processed foods, binge-watching shows, keeping our bodies idle for hours on end, etc. This is living in survival mode. But seeing life through the lens of the awakened self gives you a full range of opportunities, growth, possibilities, and awe. You break free from the distortions and learn that nothing outside of you can ever harm you, for you see that this dream is the dream you can choose to participate in, just as you would a dream at night. In your dreams, nothing can really harm you—as soon as you realize you are in the dream, then you can shift, make new choices, or change the circumstances. The same is true for our waking life. So the question becomes, what kind of dream do you really want to have? In the same way you can wake yourself up from a bad dream at night, you can steer your life experience in a new direction. You can course-correct, revise, renegotiate, and shift your awakened self from the unaware waking dream into a more pleasant state—one that feels like heaven on earth. You do this with intention and a commitment to peace, love, and compassion.

It's every person's choice how to exist and navigate the dream, but eventually we all go on a path of wanting to be our true selves fully, so we must become aware of the areas of our life that restrict this fullest expression. Over the past couple of years, several things have fallen away from my life. The more honest I am with myself and others about who I really am and what I need, it seems the more I move away from what I've known. But hiding myself is no longer an option. As Glennon Doyle says, "Anything or anyone I could lose by telling the truth was never mine anyway. I'm willing to lose anything that requires me to hide any part of myself."

I made a commitment to no longer hide behind the walls others built up for me. I will no longer allow the expectations and demands of how I should fit into this world dictate my focus. Instead, I will be me and let the world adjust. I will be who I really am instead of who others need me to be. Because when you are honest and real with yourself, you will get an honest and real reflection back. I looked around at my life and declared that I don't want to participate in the dream the world is dreaming for me anymore. I want to create my own beautiful story. With this declaration, everything shifted; I felt more joy, ease, and inner peace. This same focus can also be applied to our relationships with others.

Last summer, I encountered a situation with a friend that caused a lot of frustration. I found myself feeling helpless, and anxiety started to take over. I was trying so hard to make their troubles easier and life better for them, but they weren't accepting my help. That was when it became clear to me that I had to surrender my wishes and meet them where they were, rather than where I thought they could be. I was seeing this person's potential, but they were not living up to it. I kept feeling let down, but the solution was for me to let the situation, the person, and the world be what they were, without me projecting onto it. My dream (or hope) was not the dream they had for themselves. When we stop projecting our own version of reality onto the world, we can relax into the present moment and trust that all is as it should be. We can also trust that everyone is making choices that are best for them. I returned to my heart and asked, "What would love do?" And in that space of silence, I heard my inner voice say, *Suffering is part of the illusion.*

In Buddhism, the first Noble Truth is that all existence is characterized by suffering. There will be times in our life where we will be forced to experience the unbearable: the death of a loved one, illness, natural disasters, financial scarcity, unjust or unfair treatment, or abuse. But suffering emphasizes what the world has done to injure you. When we stay in suffering, we are forever a victim of the world, yet when we realize that the world is our dream, we can free ourselves from suffering and master our own path. Thich Nhat Hanh shares, "When another person makes you suffer, it is because he suffers deeply within himself, and his suffering is spilling over. He does not need punishment; he needs help. That's the message he is sending." What we all need is more empathy and love. We can meet the suffering and resentment that we encounter with more of the same, or we can dissolve it with compassion and light. We can dream kindnesses into being rather than dwelling on mistakes and problems.

This concept is not to say we turn a blind eye to the current realities of the world or ignore the past hurts that we've experienced. (Nor am I saying your experiences are all your fault.) The heart of this lesson is the universal truth that life is bigger and more expansive than any one thing we go through. The trying situations we face, as difficult as they can be, do not define us, because they are always growth opportunities to align us back to love. It all ties back to your deeper awareness of your soul's Divine growth. When we experience something traumatic—such as emotional, physical, or sexual abuse; domestic violence; injustice; a disease diagnosis; or even neglect or mistreatment from others—these experiences most often stay with us for years, just like a nightmare can. The pain of some life experiences gets etched into our system, and moving forward can feel impossible. Most traumatic events are incidents that make you believe you are in danger of being seriously injured or losing your life. They threaten your worldview and chop away at your safety. Although the scars, both mental and physical, will last, the point isn't to ignore or erase what you lived but to understand it.

One of the most common outcomes of trauma is avoidance, which makes sense. If you experience something traumatic, you want to avoid thinking about it or going to places that remind you of it. But to heal is to feel, and looking at our experience through the lens of Source Energy can shift our focus from hurting to healing. Have you ever noticed that Healthy Self = Heal Thy Self? I believe we are all on a journey to discover who we are and dissolve the illusions that separate us from love's true presence, which is the ultimate healing journey of our soul. I've personally been on a lifelong healing journey (as we all are)—one of self-love, truth-seeking, and increasing compassion for all things. What does your healing journey look like? Eventually our healing journeys take us to a place of ultimate surrender into service and helping each other.

I have a friend who's experienced a lifetime of continued devastations. When he was younger, his little sister committed suicide in front of him. A few years later, his brother was kidnapped, raped, tortured, and killed. Then later, his mother left the family to start a new family. After he shared his past with me, I said, "I am so sorry for all of your loss." He brushed it off, shrugged his shoulders, and said, "Thank you, but we all go through something. It's part of life. It's who we become after that matters most!" He then told me that he and his father went on to start a foundation to help children who have been missing and raise awareness about child abduction and suicide prevention. He became an activist for causes that personally affected him. Instead of suffering in his pain, he transmuted it with love and service. He could have blamed the world and let those traumas define him, but he took control of the situation by learning from it and becoming a spokesperson to help others. My friend was able to heal by practicing forgiveness and service.

> You learn to love by putting yourself in situations
> that challenge you to be loving.
>
> SANAYA ROMAN

In her book *Personal Power Through Awareness*, Sanaya Roman says, "The heart always deals with issues of trusting, opening, and reaching new levels of acceptance and understanding of others . . . forgiveness is part of unconditional love. Forgive others for all the moments they are not loving and wise."[31] You do not need to respond to the fear within others by creating it within yourself. Instead, you can become a source of healing to those around you. You attract situations into your life to learn from them. One way out and up is by responding with love. In fact, most spiritual texts and ancient wisdom teach that forgiveness is the way to freedom, especially through pain. All fear and hate are merely a lack of light and love. We can forgive others, for they know not what they do. *A Course in Miracles* shares, "Sin is a lack of love . . . The emptiness engineered by fear must be replaced by forgiveness. When people cause harm to others, it is because they have fallen away from their connection to love and divine source energy." The best thing we can do for ourselves and others is to forgive. It becomes easier to elect to forgive others when we realize that they, too, are in the illusion and trapped in fear.

---

31   Sanaya Roman, *Personal Power Through Awareness* (Tiburon, CA: HJ Kramer, 1994), 107–108.

The late Ram Dass said it best: "I can do nothing for you but work on myself . . . you can do nothing for me but to work on yourself." So, in essence, we can transform ourselves, and thus the world, by committing to our own well-being and practicing self-love and forgiveness, always.

LIFE TRUTH: IF WE CANNOT FORGIVE, WE CANNOT SEE PEACE.

My last serious romantic relationship was with a man who said he wanted to marry me, but I never really felt that it was genuine; I just sensed it was what he thought I wanted to hear. Very shortly after we broke up, he started dating another woman, and within a few months, they were engaged and soon married. Although I knew he wasn't the best long-term partner for me, I couldn't help but feel hurt by his actions and his quick ability to move on with his life. For years, I held on to the anger about our breakup. I held a grudge against him that manifested as a mistrust for all men. I didn't realize it at the time, but I needed to forgive. I thought I needed to forgive *him*, until I realized my anger was the only thing I had left of us. I was holding on to the anger as a way to keep control of a situation that felt out of control. It became clear that the person I really needed to forgive, the one I was most angry at, was myself.

Inner peace is obtained when we release the need to hold "suffering" over another or ourselves. When we forgive, we are choosing to give up control. We are surrendering to the experience of life and allowing all things to be as they are. To forgive is Divine. I recognized that I was holding a grudge toward my ex, and by forgiving, I was not only energetically freeing myself from the trappings of the situation but also helping to heal the planet. Because in forgiveness, we set ourselves free, for it is one less person suffering on the planet, one less person in pain, one less person casting judgment and ill will toward another or themselves. I could do my part by releasing the energetic hold on me. This is the purpose of peace: to activate kindness in each moment.

So who do you need to forgive? Can you free yourself from the slumbering dream state and awaken to your true self, as you are always the creator and master of the dream you choose to dream?

Let's put this lesson into practice:

To apply this lesson, Nothing Real Can Be Threatened, try these steps.

Step 1: See all things as they are, instead of as you are.

When I was early in my recovery, I went to 12 Step meetings, and the Serenity Prayer became my guiding light.

> *God, grant me the serenity to accept*
>
> *the things I cannot change,*
>
> *courage to change the things I can,*
>
> *and the wisdom to know the difference.*

In order to heal, grow, and change, we must be willing to accept things as they are and stop trying to push our own ideal onto the world. We can let the world be the world and see it for what it is: a reflection of our own internal state. When we arrive at this place of surrender, we can then actively participate in our life more fully, as we will have gained the wisdom to accept what we must allow and the courage to change the things we cannot accept. Wisdom is the ultimate life force, and it comes from a connection to your higher self.

Step 2: Awaken from the sleep state.

Suffering is removed when we choose the peace that emanates from love. When we start to truly live our lives and move from "survive" to "thrive," we activate our inner light. Nothing outside of you can harm you, except to the degree you allow it. Joseph Campbell said, "People say that what we're all seeking is a meaning for life. I don't think that's what we're really seeking. I think that what we're seeking is an experience of being alive, so that our life experiences on the purely physical plane will have resonances with our own innermost being and reality, so that we actually feel the rapture of being alive." Choosing to feel your life fully and to be present for each and every moment is the ultimate purpose and path of true serenity. Stop allowing the world to dream your dream for you—awaken to your true power and become the master creator of your own life.

Step 3: Forgive the world and yourself.
How differently will you perceive the world when you forgive all that has wronged you, including yourself? When you forgive the world of your guilt, you will be free of it. It is important to process trauma, but we can't find peace until we truly forgive. To help you forgive yourself and others, you can say this prayer from Lesson 333 in *A Course in Miracles*. (As with all passages in this book, when saying this prayer, if *Father* doesn't resonate, feel free to substitute whatever expression of the Divine works best for you.)

Forgiveness Prayer from *A Course in Miracles*

Father, forgiveness is the light You chose to shine away all conflict and all doubt, and light the way for our return to You.

Fear binds the world. Forgiveness sets it free.

A COURSE IN MIRACLES

Step 4: Actively participate in creating heaven on earth.
We all go through difficult situations, but who we become in the process is the most important thing, as we always have an opportunity to take our own experience and eventually help others—which in turn helps to uplift the entire planet. Your personal experiences are never

just about you; they impact others as well. In the Law of One, there is this message: "The best way of service to others is the constant attempt to seek to share the love of the Creator as it is known to the inner self. This involves self-knowledge and the ability to open the self to the other-self without hesitation. This involves, shall we say, radiating that which is the essence or the heart of the mind/body/spirit."[32] All of our experiences help us connect back to what is real—the infinite love of the Creator. As we advance into more self-awareness, self-trust, and love, we open up our heart and mind to be an example of unconditional love. We see that self-actualization and self-love are not selfish but part of the collective uprising, and from there, we can participate in creating heaven on earth.

You can see the world in any way you wish. But through the lens of love, you see a blissful world. You can choose to allow these blessings to be part of your everyday life, or you can choose to stay in worry, fear, and discomfort. The choice is always yours. Activate your inner light by seeing yourself as a child of Divine Love and being that love in the world. This world we live in is created for you, to experience more of who you are and play in the wonder of it all. With this sense of acceptance, you will feel lighter, freer, and more purposeful.

Questions to ask:

1. Who can I forgive?

2. How can I see through the eyes of Source Energy?

3. How can I prioritize inner peace?

4. How will I activate heaven on earth?

5. What kind of dream do I really want to live?

---

32   Don Elkins, Carla Rueckert, and James Allen McCarty, *The Ra Material: An Ancient Astronaut Speaks* (Atglen, PA: Whitford Press, 1984).

Whenever anxiety takes over and fear sets in, I return to the wisdom of this lesson. I use the lesson as a mantra and repeat, "Nothing real can be threatened." As I repeat these words, my body is filled with love, and a soft, warm glow washes over me. The worry is replaced with peace, and my fear is removed with my recognition of the truth.

In the next and final lesson, you will learn how to activate the full aspect of your true nature—your unshakable inner peace—and step into your truest power. We will put all the lessons together and discover how everything is connected, because love is truly all there is. Think of the next lesson as your completion, a master ceremony bringing you into ultimate inner peace and awakened living. I will take you through the final barrier keeping us from experiencing life fulfillment and ultimate freedom: our resistance to love. Together we will remove any lingering sabotage keeping you from the ultimate Life Truth that Love Is All There Is.

LESSON 11

LOVE IS ALL THERE IS

The first week of November 2020 was incredibly intense throughout the entire world. In many countries, the global pandemic was increasing its hold, with stricter lockdown and testing measures for COVID-19. Intense earthquakes destroyed portions of cities in countries such as Turkey and Greece, destructive floods rampaged in Central America, and terrorist attacks occurred in Paris and Vienna—along with worldwide protests, civil unrest, police brutality, threatened human rights, and the heated American presidential election, which carried on for days. When we looked out into the world, it was all too much to bear. We were living through extreme chaos and mass confusion. With so much despair across the planet, it seemed impossible to find inner peace; but during this turbulent time, I experienced something very different than expected. Even though the world seemed to be in complete chaos, I was at complete peace. The contrast I saw outside of me only served to reveal more clarity within.

During this time, I went for a walk one day with my dog, and I saw my neighbor. I asked how she was doing, and she looked as though she was on the verge of tears. Her eyes were puffy and red; I assumed she had been crying. "Not good," she responded, grave concern in her voice. She said she hadn't slept in days, as she had been glued to the TV, waiting for the news to tell her the fate of the American future in the form of the election results. She wasn't eating, and her skin was dry and splotchy. These are all classic signs of extreme stress, and all of this stress had been caused by her intense focus on the things she couldn't control—which only made her feel more helpless, hopeless, and full of despair.

I knew firsthand what she was going through because I used to live my life that way as well: always stressed out and worried about the things I couldn't control, looking to the outside world to tell me things would be okay instead of discovering reassurance within. It was a difficult way to go through each day. I always felt as if I was fighting an uphill battle. I could see her struggle clearly, but when you are in that kind of extreme stress, it can be hard to calm down. When we are in a heighted state of worry and consumed with fear, our physical stress levels will always sky-rocket, which can cloud our judgment and force out logic and reason.

The ego loves to be validated, and focusing on what we can't control gives us a sense of control. One of the ways it does this is by *trauma bonding*. When people experience traumatic experiences together, they are often more likely to be connected and bonded. This can often create a codependent and unhealthy relationship. But trauma bonding can also happen on an energetic, emotional level. Being consumed with worry and fear is a bit like being in an abusive relationship with ourselves. In the traditional sense, trauma bonding is loyalty to a person who is destructive—but how many of us are actually loyal to our own destructive thoughts, choosing to defend them even when others suggest that we may be looking at things from a skewed perspective? When we hook into fear and worry, we are falling down a destructive path. We feel more helpless, and this creates even more intense inse-curities. We become dependent on these emotions because we falsely believe they are giving us security and control—but this just invites more destruction.

This loyalty to our destructive thoughts isn't restricted to just worries about the world but also includes the insecurities and limiting beliefs we hide behind. The nature of a trauma bond is that it makes the per-son unable to see reality, themselves, or situations clearly. When we are consumed with worry or trapped by a limiting belief, we are blinded to solutions. We can't think clearly or optimize our options. This is a form of self-sabotage, because we've been conditioned to believe that we're not going to get safety or peace unless we worry about it. Our negative thoughts of worry, doubt (including self-doubt), insecurity, and fear don't make us feel good, yet we hold on to them with the belief that we can worry our way out of the troubling situation.

There is a way out of the worry cycle, though. It is a matter of choice. Each individual always has a choice. Your ego knows this, and it thrives on your codependency with worry and fear, making you believe you don't have a choice. In my conversation with my neighbor, it seemed she was inviting me to join her in this focus on fear. She asked, "How are you not worried? The world is going to hell." I felt compassion and empathy for her, but I knew that being worried about the world would not help me feel good, so I smiled softly and gently said, "Well, that is one way to look at it, but I am choosing to focus on possibilities and what is on the other side of all this chaos. I am looking for the love and beauty on Earth." She asked, "How is there beauty in such destruction and chaos? Why are you not scared?" I said, "I'm not scared because I trust God, and I know we will prevail. We always do. Humans are resilient, and even though the world is being turned upside down, it's giving us the opportunity to re-align with and connect to what matters most." It's a matter of choice. We get to choose—do we want to align with heaviness or hope? Fear or faith? Worry or wonder? Lack or love?

> Our level of love or our level of fear
> determines the state of our reality.
>
> STEPHEN RICHARDS

As Abraham Hicks said, "If it doesn't feel good, it's not going to feel any better by thinking about it longer." The more we fester in frustration and angst, the harder it is to see a way out of the emotional turmoil. Everything comes back to how we perceive situations. We will always feel more peace when we can look at our experiences as an opportunity for us to grow into more love and activate the light within each one of our hearts. In watching how distraught my neighbor was, I knew it wasn't my place to try to change her or pull her out of her emotional state. Sometimes, we need to be in a state of worry in order to discover what we care about the most. There are times still when I worry, fall into grave concern, and even have moments of panic, but I no longer fester in this space. What used to last years, months, or weeks is now a few hours or less. I catch myself, but also allow myself to feel it all. Part of living a magnificent life is to be present for all that is revealed. Allow yourself to dive deep into the journey of your life. Acknowledge all that comes into your experience of life. Allow it, let it be, then release it once you've understood it. Our pain has a purpose to it. It is not about pushing it away but diving into it to be present with it so it can heal and reveal more love. What heals trauma? Love. Love is the only answer, and all there truly is.

The intensity of emotion surrounding the 2020 presidential election showed up within my inner circle as well. I had a group of friends who voted differently than my family did, so I found myself in between two totally opposite text chains. For myself, I took a new approach to everything surrounding the election: I remained neutral and unattached to the outcome. I knew that from a spiritual perspective, the outcome that was certain was the one that was for the highest good for all involved because everything is always in Divine Order. But what I witnessed from each text chain was total opposition and attack. Anytime a candidate was in the lead, the group that didn't want that candidate to win would blame, point fingers, and cast judgment. Each group would attack the other candidate and their supporters. When they asked me to chime in, I said, "I don't want to participate in separation. I am sending immense love to both candidates and trust the outcome that is certain is the one that will be for the highest good of all humanity." I knew we had a choice to either focus on love and see the good in all or focus on anger, worry or fear.

Knowing that there is a Divine Order to everything is not about surrendering your will and giving up, nor is it about being complicit, naïve, or attempting to spiritually bypass. It's about aligning with your faith, which is stronger than fear. It's about reclaiming your true power by refusing to let the world hijack your attention and emotions. It is about connecting to your true nature, the one of an unshakable inner peace. This peace gives you a deep inner knowing that love will always prevail. This truth is irreplaceable, and you feel it. You feel how good it is to be in this space of peace, and you no longer want to participate in the fear and drama of the outside world. There are a lot of things we can't control, so worrying about them only keeps us trapped in a frantic mental state. Reclaim your energy and life force, and focus on what feels good: joy, love, peace, kindness, etc. There are a lot of distractions and fear in the world, and when we give our attention to these outside forces, we lose sight of our authentic power. You have the power to live in harmony and peace, but it depends on how you show up for yourself and others.

Look at any area in your life where you are resisting, blaming, or judging. Are you pushing against what you fear and lashing out energetically? We live in a system that thrives on pushing us apart and keeping us separate from one another. Don't fall into this trap. We need each other, differences and all. Look at the separations in your life, and make a commitment to bring more unity, compassion, and understanding to each situation and relationship.

You know intuitively that this separation from others who see things differently isn't working. It isn't in your true nature. The true you—your spirit and best human self—needs connection and unity. The mission at hand is to love everything and accept it for what and where it is. Love it all, because everything is made from love.

LIFE TRUTH: EVERYTHING IS ALWAYS IN DIVINE ORDER.

What often blocks us from love is judgment. When things feel uncertain, we can fall into the form of worry that is judgment. There was a phase of my life in which judgment reared its ugly head in conversations with friends and family. I noticed a lot of people I talked to often making comments about others. My friend explained that she had run into someone we hadn't seen in years and told me how much weight she had gained and how she had let herself go. I found myself feeling defensive and mad at my friend for judging our childhood friend based on her looks. As time passed, I began to notice how common these types of judgments were in my conversations, and then I realized that I too was judging them—for judging others' physical appearance. Every time a friend had an opinion based on someone else's physical appearance, I would get frustrated and triggered because when I look at people, I don't define them by their physical attributes or what society deems faults. I look for their truth and see their inner light. But with each friend or family member who made comments and judgments about others, I would secretly judge them myself (which meant just more of the same because I was participating in the problem). But when I held up the energetic mirror and asked, "How is this a reflection of my internal state?" it became clear that most of my judgment was actually at myself. When I realized this pattern was keeping me away from love, I relinquished it. Lesson 352 in *A Course in Miracles* says, "Judgment and love are opposites. From one comes all the sorrows of the world, but from the other comes the peace of God Himself." In the face of judgment, I created a mini prayer to reestablish my connection to love.

A Prayer to Release Judgment

I see my judgment.

I recognize this as an imbalance of my true self.

I realign with love and see all as the same.

I stand firm in my truth.

When we align with the love within us, we feel better and we are more grounded. We aren't hung up on projections or insecurities because we are connected to a source of infinite Divine power.

I've come to believe that the biggest barrier to reaching inner peace is our resistance to love. So often we push away that which we really need and want. In my own journey, I saw this play out in my personal life. I started to open up to the idea of being in a relationship again, yet I kept meeting people who were cookie-cutter versions of people and patterns I thought I had healed from and moved past. I kept meeting men with similar habits, unhealed wounds, and patterns, which of course created the same push-pull that I had experienced with previous relationships. I had to ask myself, "Why do I keep attracting men who are wrong for me and emotionally unavailable?" By asking this question, it became clear to me that it was because I was still emotionally unavailable. The men I met were mirrors of my own resistance to love. I knew I needed to change my focus if I wanted a new outcome. I had been focusing so much on not getting hurt. I had been trying to protect myself, and I approached each new person through the lens of mistrust. You can imagine how well that worked out. Every new date and encounter turned into more frustration and hopelessness.

As it turned out, I needed to change my goal. My goal had been to not get hurt, but that just kept bringing more disappointments to me. I realigned with my ultimate purpose by asking myself this question from Glennon Doyle: "What is the desire behind the desire?" And my ultimate desire was to be loved and seen for who I am. I wanted to live a fulfilling life alongside a partner who was also dedicated to the same. So I refocused my intent, and this changed my entire experience. Something beautiful happened.

I had recently reconnected with someone from my past, and there had been an insane instant connection. At first this scared me, so I pushed him away. I was trying to see how he fit into my life, but I kept resisting his attempts to be together as I tried to control our outcome. It wasn't until I shifted my perception from "How can he fit into my current life?" to "How can I grow into a new life?" that things changed, as I accepted him and the love being presented to me. I surrendered to the experience available for me. Expansion, growth, joy, companionship, and love are waiting for us. We have to allow, accept, and receive them. I needed to find new balance, one that embraced and welcomed in all forms of love.

Sometimes to lose balance for love
is part of living a balanced life.

ELIZABETH GILBERT

Love is all there is; we either resist or accept it. We invite it in and live with this grace, and we trust that what feels good is more important than what looks good. We either stay safe and secure or expand into new growth and life-changing experiences. Let yourself lead with love. It is the reason we are here.

When we change the goal, we get new outcomes. Is your current reality driven by a focus derived from fear? Mine certainly was. Not wanting to get hurt is a pretty sad goal, if you ask me. I wasn't focusing on what I wanted, just on what I didn't want. But in realigning with love and removing my resistance to it, I welcomed new love into my life through a new partnership. Although we aren't together anymore, it was a beautiful gift to let love in. Love shows up in all forms, and it is all around us at all times. We just have to commit to removing our resistance to love's presence and let life in. Because living a big, beautiful, brave life is love in action. Perhaps our focus can shift—we can see that love truly is all there is, including the love we hold and have for ourselves, and the knowing that we are enough and have everything we need.

To further demonstrate this truth, we can look to ancient texts and wise mystics of the ages. In the Pleiadean Light Forces transmission, Michael Love shares the Four Core Principles of Love,[33] which is the master teaching that all great wisdom written in the ancient spiritual and religious books ultimately originated from.

The Principles of Love:

1. Love is the inherent, primary nature of the Universe.

2. Love is the highest vibrational and most powerful energy in the Universe.

3. You are this Love.

4. Realize and be what you truly are.

---

33 Michael Love, "Pleiadean Master Teachings—Light Forces Transmissions," April 13, 2021, YouTube video, youtube.com/watch?v=dRwL4-58GTg&t. (Principles are mentioned at 7:30 timestamp and 10:02 timestamp.)

After we realize our true identity, the goal is to start being this. Be love in action. Vibrate love from your every pore. See love, be love, give love, and receive love. We can activate these four core principles of love in every situation of our life, and when we do, we live from a place of balance, truth, integrity, and peace.

For the past decade, I've had a dear friend who has also been my life coach and guru. Summer Bacon, who works with Dr. Peebles, had been my constant support, but several months before I finished writing this book, she canceled my coaching sessions along with those of all her other clients and publicly announced her early retirement. Shocked, mad, and extremely frustrated, I spent weeks trying to process our partnership ending. Her mentorship and guidance had helped me overcome clinical depression, eating disorders, and a lack of self-love—and to discover my true passion and purpose as a writer and coach. I attributed the majority of my clear direction and success to their unwavering support. I even dedicated my last book to them. To have this ripped away so suddenly felt like a giant freefall.

I spent weeks feeling out of sorts and was consumed with judgment toward my dear friend, who had abandoned her clients when we needed her most. At least that was what I kept telling myself, until I recalled everything I'd just been writing about and decided to practice the lessons in this book. I took the lessons one by one and applied them to my situation, and soon things shifted. In doing so, I realized how special it was for her to finally take care of herself first—the ultimate form of self-love and care. You see, it's all about love, and love for self is first and foremost for our ultimate peace and joy. After twenty-five years of helping others and being of service to so many people, she was finally putting herself first. I also recognized that the more I energetically attacked her with judgmental thoughts, the less credit I was giving to her and myself and all the work we had done together over the years. It became painfully obvious that now was the time to put all of the guidance I had received into full force. It was time to be my own guru and coach.

When I surrendered to this new reality, I felt limitless. I replaced my anger with love. I stepped into a place of appreciation and trusted that all was in the right order. In sending love to my coach, I felt lighter, more relaxed, and peaceful. I remembered that we are in a school called planet Earth and our souls have seasons. I recognized that everyone is on their own journey, that our purpose is to expand, and that in order to receive, we must release. I reminded myself that nothing real can be threatened and love truly is all there is. With peace and love as my focus, not only did things become easier but, as I wrote this chapter, I received an email from my dear friend and decade-long coach. She announced that she was not retiring after all—she just realized she needed a break for self-love and care. When I read the words, I cried tears of joy. Love had united us, as it does everything. Love is all there is, and anger, fear, worry, concern, and judgment will always come into our experience to give us an opportunity to return to love. Love is the healer, the elixir, and the power potion that we all desperately need. But it isn't outside of us. Love is within us, for it is us.

> Whatever the question is,
> the answer is always more love.
>
> LEE CARROLL

We are here on Earth at a very unique time, and now more than ever, we are starting to see that we have more power than we've ever known. It is our highest path to return to this sacred truth that you are magnificent and sourced from the highest vibration in the Universe: love. Even though we might be able to conceptualize this, it can be easy to fall into worry and get trapped in the illusions of separation. Through our life experiences, struggles, setbacks, goals, and dreams, we are gifted the opportunity to return to love—the ultimate true you—which is the way forward. We access this love by aligning with our true set point: peace. Peace is your personal power and the way through all blocks. As Summer Bacon and Dr. Peebles say, we are all part of the Universal Alliance for Global Peace.

You've chosen to read this book for the same reason you choose to be here on Earth at this magnificent time: to bring more light and love into the world by aligning with your true nature: the peace and love within. You have a mission, and you've been given all the tools to activate this fully. The lessons presented in this book serve as a blueprint for conscious creative living. They can be your source of inspiration in times of trouble, your energy when you lack motivation, and your guide when you see confusion. As I've said before, *Return to You* is about an unshakable inner peace. This isn't just a book to read or fun mantra to say. Rather, it is your purpose—to be the light and allow and accept the love that you truly are. You are doing your part to help yourself, which helps those around you and, in turn, helps to uplift the planet.

LIFE TRUTH: WHEN YOU CONNECT TO YOUR TRUE POWER—THE LOVE WITHIN—YOU BECOME A BEACON OF LIGHT, WHICH HELPS TO TRANSFORM THE ENTIRE PLANET.

My commitment with this book is to help you connect to your true power, the love within and all around you. With this connection, you discover the unshakable inner peace that is your birthright, and you are guided to your true purpose: to be the love that you are and share it with others. By reading this book and living the lessons shared, you are now part of the Universal Alliance for Global Peace. What does this mean? It means you make your choices inspired from a place of your true nature; you choose love because you know with every fiber of your being that you are here to be love, receive love, and spread love. You know you make a profound impact in this world by being yourself and shining your light. Thank you for showing up so fully for yourself. The world needs you and your light. Never forget that peace is your purpose and that the light within you is your true power.

LIFE TRUTH: PEACE IS YOUR TRUTH.

Let's put this lesson into practice:

To activate this lesson, Love Is All There Is, try these steps.

Step 1: Accept the love available to you.

Accept the love in your life—whether that is through a romantic partner, the joy of your job, a passion, a connection with pleasure and living life more fully, or a connection with the spiritual world and Source Energy—whatever you choose, love is all around us. Accept the love by opening your heart and giving yourself permission to receive. Receiving isn't just about you; it's about the other person, too. When you give of your time, money, and energy, you share yourself with the world, and this is the joy of giving. It goes both ways. What would it be like for you to look at receiving differently? This is also linked to loving ourselves. Can you be open and allow people to give to you? Open your heart and stay committed to love. Let love guide you, lead you, and support you. Celebrate who you are, which is a beautiful person worthy of receiving, being, and giving love.

Step 2: Make peace your purpose.

Peace is available to you when you allow yourself to be who you really are. Peace is your purpose, and it is part of living a fulfilled life. You don't have to change yourself or try to fit in the world. You simply open up to your Divine Self and let the world be what it is. You can lead a life of wonder and awe with peace as your purpose.

Step 3: Return to you.

It has always been and will always be about love. Love is the highest and most powerful vibrational energy in the Universe, and it is you. The love that you are, the love that is possible for you, the love you can receive, and the love that you have to give to yourself and the world—this is your true nature. Return to you, the love that is inside you and has been there all along. This is your true power and purpose.

Questions to ask:

1. How can I bring more peace to all I do?

2. How will I show more love to myself and the world?

It has always and only been about love.

THE UNIVERSE

RESOURCES

RETURN TO YOU JOURNAL PROMPTS

An important part of reaching self-awareness and inner peace is self-inquiry. One of the best ways that I've found to do this is by journaling, which is why I created this section to help you answer the main questions presented throughout this book. These strategic questions will help you reclaim your personal power and return to you. Pull out a pen and paper, and enjoy the journey inward.

Lesson 1: You Are in a School Called Planet Earth

1. What is the lesson and course I am currently in?

2. How can I participate more fully in my own growth and inner expansion?

3. How have I learned through the contrast, and what is true for me?

Lesson 2: If You Don't Go Within, You Go Without

4. What is my intuition style, and how will I grow my connection to it?

5. How's the outside world mirroring my inner world?

6. Where do I feel called to help and be of service to others?

Lesson 3: Faith Is Freedom from Fear

7. How can I focus more on the moment and appreciate all that is going well?

8. How can I relinquish control of the situation causing me the most stress?

9. What is my fear, anxiety, worry, or discomfort trying to show me?

10. How can I reclaim my power?

11. What is my faith asking of me?

Lesson 4: Your Beliefs Create Your Reality

12. Why did this person say what they are saying?
    a. What is their belief (worldview) that is creating this reality for them?
    b. Is there truth in what they are saying?
    c. If there is no truth, then why am I angry?
    d. Can I transform this situation with more love and forgiveness?

13. Which people, places, beliefs, habits, and situations are supporting me and my growth, and which ones are limiting?

14. How can I detach from drama and align with my inner light?

15. What belief, pattern, or habit is no longer serving me?

Lesson 5: Everyone Is on Their Own Journey

16. How can I release all judgment, comparison, and shame and focus more on my own path?

17. Can I give myself more credit for all of the amazing things I've done?

18. How can I be kind, compassionate, and loving to myself and others?

19. Which relationships feel strained, and which ones need more attention and care?

Lesson 6: Your Soul Has Seasons

20. What am I clinging to or restricting?

21. What is no longer serving me or my highest good?

22. What is no longer in alignment and needs to change?

23. What is the future I am working to create?

24. What inspiration is coming to me?

25. What guiding action can I take today to help build the future I want?

26. What does the true me need and want?

27. What am I grateful for, and what can I celebrate?

28. In what new ways do I want to express myself?

29. How can I show up for myself in ways I never have before?

30. How can I be more intentional with my choices and live with more purpose?

31. What kind of life do I really want to live?

32. Who have I become? Who do I want to be?

Lesson 7: Your Purpose Is Personal Expansion

33. How can I be more intentional with my choices and live more on purpose?

34. Where am I being called to serve and support others?

35. Where is my heart guiding me, and what guided action can I take today?

36. How can I actively participate in creating a more harmonious world?

Lesson 8: In Order to Receive, You Must Release

37. How can I build a more positive relationship with my body and listen to and understand more of its needs?

38. What battle within myself am I committed to healing?

39. Do I believe we live in a hostile or friendly Universe?

40. What do I want to release?

41. What am I ready to receive?

Lesson 9: The Universe Rewards Motion

42. How can I trust myself more?

43. What synchronicities have I experienced recently?

44. What guided action can I take today?

45. Where do I still seek validation or approval from outside sources, and how can I instead validate and approve of myself?

Lesson 10: Nothing Real Can Be Threatened

46. Who can I forgive?

47. How can I see through the eyes of Source Energy?

48. How can I prioritize inner peace?

49. How will I activate heaven on earth?

50. What kind of dream do I really want to live?

Lesson 11: Love Is All There Is

51. How can I bring more peace to all I do?

52. How will I show more love to myself and the world?

MANTRAS

Mantras (or affirmations) are a powerful way to retrain the brain to focus on feeling good. You can connect to peace in each moment by reaffirming these Life Truths. These are the mantras shared throughout this process and book.

"I am peace. Peace is within me. Peace is all around me."

"I release all fear that tries to tells me I should be somewhere different from where I actually am."

"I focus on faith and trust the process. I welcome the unknown because it represents growth."

"Let me be still and listen to the truth."

"In this moment, I am safe and secure."

"I am a child of Source Energy, love, God, etc. My power is in my connection to the Divine."

"I am willing to see the love available to me in this experience."

"My thoughts about my deepest fears are not my reality. They are illusions separating me from love."

"All contrast brings more clarity."

"I choose the joy of God instead of pain."

"I disengage from all illusions. I am not separate from my truth. I am love."

"I am willing to accept the perfect love of the Creator."

"I am willing to release this relationship with peace and harmony."

"I thank you for our relationship. I release you with love."

"Peace is my truth."

PRAYERS

Prayer is one of the best ways to realign yourself with the Divine Source Energy. These are the prayers shared throughout this process and book.

A Prayer for Discernment

Dear Source,

Please guide me to the path of least resistance and optimal alignment. Please help me see the truth and connect to the outcome that is for the highest good of all involved.

A Prayer for Peace

I detach from anything that seeks to separate.

Anything that says "Us versus them."

Anything that says "My way or the highway."

Anything that seeks to destroy, condemn, shame, or blame.

Instead, I choose unity.

I choose kindness, compassion.

I choose love.

Forgiveness Prayer from
A Course in Miracles

*Father, forgiveness is the light You chose to shine away all
conflict and all doubt, and light the way for our return to You.*

A Prayer to Release Judgment

I see my judgment.

I recognize this as an imbalance of my true self.

I realign with love and see all as the same.

I stand firm in my truth.

Serenity Prayer

God, grant me the serenity to accept

the things I cannot change,

courage to change the things I can,

and wisdom to know the difference.

A Prayer for Releasing Your Attachment to the Body

*I am not a body. I am Free. For I am still as God created
me. I feel the Love of God within me now. The Love of
God is what created me. The Love of God is everything I
am . . . The Love of God within me sets me Free.*

MEDITATIONS

Guided Meditation to Alchemize Fear

Step 1: Identify Your Fear
Start by feeling the fear and sitting with it. The things you are afraid of can be your greatest teacher. Name your fear. What is the fear at the center of your current experience? Fear of being judged, not being loved, not being accepted, dying, losing loved ones, etc.? Identify the fear, and call it out specifically.

- Where does it live in your body?
- What does it feel like and look like?

Really feel into the fear, and be present with how it feels. By identifying it, you no longer run from it or allow it to control your experience.

Step 2: Step into Your Fear
Imagine this fear engulfed by a tornado of energy. The fear is now circling and rotating fiercely all around you. The fear has become a tornado of energy. Step into the center of the tornado, and allow this fear to override everything in its natural, frantic pace around you. Do this visualization and energy work until you are at the peak of the fear. Really feel the intensity.

- What does it feel like?
- What emotions are coming up?
- What is your natural response to this experience?

Do you want to run, fight back, hide, etc.? This is an indication of where your power lives, or lack of power—where you've been giving it away.

Step 3: Understand Your Fear

The next step is to stay present, centered in the middle of the tornado of energy and frantic fear, and understand it. You do this by working with it and communicating to release its energetic hold on and power over you. Stand in the tornado, and really feel the movement and energy. As you do, stand firm in the center, and ask the fear these questions.

- What message do you have for me?
- What are you here to teach me?

Step 4: Transcend Your Fear

This next step will help you embody this fear. Understand that this fear is an illusion. It is a false identity and thought form that has been given to you from outside of your true self. Take your power back by aligning with your truth. In this space, stand firm in the center of the tornado of fear, repeat three truths, and in between each truth, repeat, "I disengage from all illusions. I am not separate from my truth. I am love."

It looks something like this (although you will create and repeat your own truths):

Truth one: "In this moment, I am safe and secure."

Mantra: "I disengage from all illusions. I am not separate from my truth. I am love."

Take a deep breath in and out.

Truth two: "I am willing to see the love available to me in this experience."

Mantra: "I disengage from all illusions. I am not separate from my truth. I am love."

Take a deep breath in and out.

Truth three: "I am a child of Source Energy, Love, God, etc. My power is in my connection to the Divine."

Mantra: "I disengage from all illusions. I am not separate from my truth. I am love."

Take a deep breath in and out.

As you do this visualization and energetic meditation, breathe in and out deeply between each truth statement.

Your truth is your power. When you actively participate in disengaging with emotions that are bringing you down, you can reclaim your power and help to uplift not only yourself but the entire world.

* This meditation is inspired by an original teaching in the book *Busting Loose from the Money Game* by Robert Scheinfeld.

Releasing Relationships Meditation
(For When Things Just Feel Off)

If you want to leave or change a relationship, you can work on a
soul level to ensure both of you go in peace, love, and harmony.
Close your eyes and imagine the person standing next to you.
Imagine that you have been walking along a path together,
and now the path is dividing. There is a fork in the road.
It is in your highest good for both of you
to go forth on your respective paths.
Know that each one of you has become more of who
you are supposed to be and must now concentrate on
this new route for optimal growth and awareness.
Pay attention to how you feel in this moment of
parting. Get in touch with your true feelings.
Trust the process, and release this person with love.
It is necessary for you to grow and evolve past each other
in different directions for you to each get what you need.
There is no need to see this as an ending, but
rather focus on the new beginning.
See the relationship as a success. Reflect on all the experiences
you created together. Celebrate the relationship with love.
Be willing to release the other person and
allow each other to go your own way.
Send this person love, and repeat the mantra "I thank
you for our relationship. I release you with love."

* This meditation and concept are inspired by *Soul Love: Awaken Your Heart Centers* by Sanaya Roman.

Vibrational Healing Meditation for Body Peace

Repeat these words as you do this activation meditation:
"Dear Universal support system of love and light, please remove all negative energy, thoughts, and perceptions directed at me or within me."
Next, visualize the energy of your higher self as a most glorious golden-white light pouring in through the top of your head.
Picture the white crystalized light flooding your entire body with warm, loving presence and flushing through your whole being. As the light touches each cell, it transforms it into pure health and ultimate vibrancy.
See the white light soothing all of your cells and activating their highest potential.
Feel the energy flush through you as it transforms all disharmony and discomfort.
Repeat these words aloud three times:
"I acknowledge the light within me. I accept the perfect love that I am. I am whole. I am love."

ACKNOWLEDGMENTS

There are many people who helped make this book possible and for whom I am eternally grateful. My literary agents Steve Harris at CSG Literary Partners and Michele Martin at MDM Management: you've been with me since the beginning of my author career, and I'm so grateful for your continued enthusiasm and consistent partnership. To my personal editor, Brianne Bardusch: thank you for your professionalism, commitment, and focus on all my projects. To my editor at Sounds True, Diana Ventimiglia: I am so glad we get to bring this project out into the world. Thank you for believing in me and seeing this vision into life. To the entire Sounds True team, from production to marketing, of this book and the *Unshakable Inner Peace Oracle Cards* deck: thank you for your commitment to a more awakened and aligned world, and thank you for adding me to your team of spiritual teachers and authors. Thank you to my family for believing in me and always being by my side—your support and unconditional love is unwavering, and I love you. Thank you to my friends Marita, Stacey, and Amy: you are soul sisters. Thank you to my teachers and mentors who helped inform this book and make this teaching possible: Summer Bacon and Dr. Peebles, Lee Carol and Kryon, Paul Selig and the Guides, Sanaya Roman and Orin, and Esther Hicks and Abraham. Thank you, Universal Source Energy, the Divine, God, and my Guides. And to those of you in my Play with the World community and @ShannonKaiserWrites community, I am grateful for your passion for life and commitment to inner peace and joy. This book serves as an advancement in my core teachings, and I am honored you are still with me on this journey. And to you, dear reader: thank you for your commitment to a life of growth, new awareness, and inner peace. It is an honor to support you on your journey. And to planet Earth, Gaia, Mother Nature: I appreciate you and all you do for humanity. Thank you for being our home as we evolve and grow. I honor your wisdom and healing power. And last but not least, thanks to Chance, my golden retriever rescue dog. What an epic life adventure we are on together. Thanks for making every day full of so much love and joy.

ABOUT THE AUTHOR

Shannon Kaiser is the bestselling author of five books on the psychology of happiness and fulfillment, including the #1 bestseller *The Self-Love Experiment*, as well as *Adventures for Your Soul, Find Your Happy Daily Mantras,* and *Joy Seeker,* and is the creator of the *Unshakable Inner Peace Oracle Cards* deck. As an international empowerment coach, author, business mentor, speaker, and retreat leader, she guides people to awaken and align with their authentic self so they can live the life they are made for. She's been named among the "100 Women to Watch in Wellness" by mindbodygreen and "your-go-to happiness booster" by *Health* magazine. She has also been recognized as a Must-Follow Instagram Account for Inspiration by *Entrepreneur* magazine and a Top Facebook Account for Daily Motivation by mindbodygreen. Visit her website at playwiththeworld.com, and follow her on social media @ShannonKaiserWrites.

ABOUT SOUNDS TRUE

Sounds True is a multimedia publisher whose mission is to inspire and support personal transformation and spiritual awakening. Founded in 1985 and located in Boulder, Colorado, we work with many of the leading spiritual teachers, thinkers, healers, and visionary artists of our time. We strive with every title to preserve the essential "living wisdom" of the author or artist. It is our goal to create products that not only provide information to a reader or listener but also embody the quality of a wisdom transmission.

For those seeking genuine transformation, Sounds True is your trusted partner. At SoundsTrue.com you will find a wealth of free resources to support your journey, including exclusive weekly audio interviews, free downloads, interactive learning tools, and other special savings on all our titles.

To learn more, please visit SoundsTrue.com/freegifts or call us toll-free at 800.333.9185.

sounds true

WAKING UP THE WORLD